A FAMILY CHRONICLE

MENDEL'S CHILDREN

Mendel Steiman

A FAMILY CHRONICLE

MENDEL'S CHILDREN

CHERIE SMITH

University of Calgary Press

University of Calgary Press
2500 University Drive, N.W.
Calgary, Alberta T2N 1N4

CANADIAN CATALOGUING IN PUBLICATION DATA

Smith, Cherie, 1933-
    Mendel's children

    Includes bibliographical references.
    ISBN 1-895176-85-9

    1. Steiman family. 2. Shatsky family. 3. Finn family. 4.
Jews—Saskatchewan—Kamsack Region—Biography. 5.
Pioneers—Saskatchewan—Kamsack Region—Biography. 6.
Frontier and pioneer life—Saskatchewan—Kamsack Region.
7. Kamsack Region (Sask.)—History. I. Title.
FC3549.K34Z48 1997   971.24'2004924   C97-910683-4
F1074.5.K34S64 1997

Design & composition by Eric Ansley & Associates Ltd.
Maps by Henry Meyer
Printed and bound in Canada on acid-free paper.
Selections from this book, in slightly different versions, first appeared in Canadian Woman Studies, Canadian Ethnic Studies and Saskatchewan History.

COMMITTED TO THE DEVELOPMENT OF CULTURE AND THE ARTS

For *Connie* and *Gary*
and my grandchildren
Graeme, Laura and Donald

. . . memory believes
before knowing remembers.
David Quammen

I am the family face;
flesh perishes,
I live on.
Thomas Hardy

Trees have roots;
Jews have legs.
Isaac Deutscher

Contents

AUTHOR'S NOTE

This book has been a labour of love. It led me to the archives of the Institute for Jewish Research in New York, to Latvia and the USSR where I found long-lost relatives, and to Winnipeg where I made contact with family and friends I had not seen since I left in 1945.

It was never my intention to attempt to write a definitive chronicle of my clan and, as an untrained historian, I have in some instances invoked the storyteller's licence.

In my ten-year search for information, memories, photographs and newspaper clippings, many relatives and friends helped me — Marcie Smordin, Doris Gould, Marion Katz, Esther Matas and especially Gerry Baker as well as Lily and Manuel Morry, Dora Zaslovsky, Boris, Maxwell and Lionel Steiman.

I am profoundly indebted to my mentor, Jacob Zilber, for his generous advice and encouragement over the years; to Kenneth Dyba, David Evanier, Elizabeth and David Morantz; to Vulf Sternin and Frank Fox for checking the Russian history; to Mary Anne Morel and Norma Gutteridge, who were instrumental in getting the book published.

My thanks to Bonnie Tregebov of the Jewish Historical Society of Western Canada; Lynn Champagne Cormack of the Manitoba Archives; and last, but not least, my husband Julian, who put up with my obsession with great patience and good humour, encouraging me always.

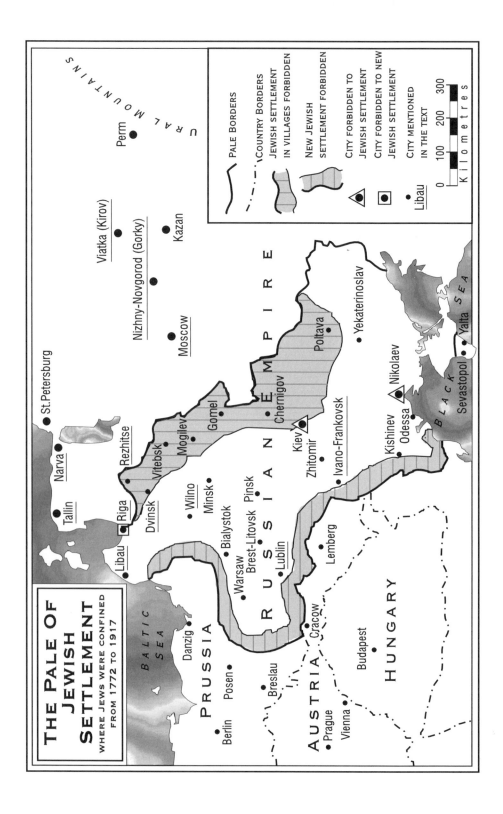

THE PALE OF JEWISH SETTLEMENT

WHERE JEWS WERE CONFINED FROM 1772 TO 1917

Legend:

PALE BORDERS

COUNTRY BORDERS

JEWISH SETTLEMENT IN VILLAGES FORBIDDEN

NEW JEWISH SETTLEMENT FORBIDDEN

CITY FORBIDDEN TO JEWISH SETTLEMENT

CITY FORBIDDEN TO NEW JEWISH SETTLEMENT

Libau   CITY MENTIONED IN THE TEXT

Kilometres: 0 100 200 300

Labels:

URAL MOUNTAINS

Perm

Viatka (Kirov)

Nizhny-Novgorod (Gorky)

Kazan

Moscow

St.Petersburg

Narva

Tallin

Rezhitse

Riga

Vitebsk

Dvinsk

Libau

Wilno

Minsk

Bialystok

Brest-Litovsk

Pinsk

Warsaw

Lublin

Mogilev

Gomel

Chernigov

Poltava

Yekaterinoslav

Nikolaev

Kiev

Zhitomir

Ivano-Frankovsk

Kishinev

Odessa

Sevastopol

Yalta

Lemberg

Cracow

Budapest

Danzig

Posen

Breslau

Berlin

Prague

Vienna

R U S S I A N   E M P I R E

PRUSSIA

AUSTRIA

HUNGARY

BALTIC SEA

BLACK SEA

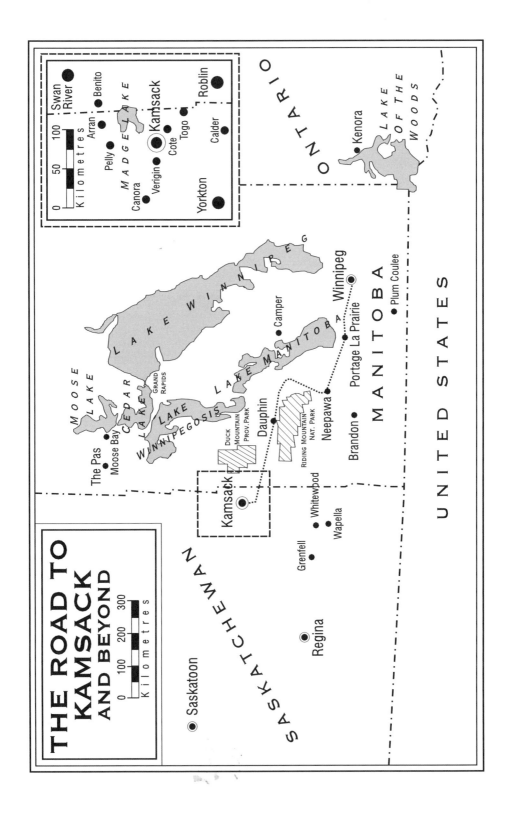

THE ROAD TO
KAMSACK
AND BEYOND

Kilometres
0   100   200   300

The Steiman Family

Dova

Jacob
Steiman

Mordichai
Steiman

Mendel
Steiman
1846–1924

=

Solomon
Steiman
1863–1942

=

Etza
Feigelson
1875–1939

Boris
Steiman
1919–1995

=

Molly
Spevack
1920–

Lily
Steiman
1895–1985

=

Saul
Morry
1899–1959

Iser
Steiman
1898–1981

=

Laura
Shatsky
1904–1986

Mark
Steiman
1900–1942

=

Faina
Frierman

Dora
Steiman
1905–1996

=

Meyer
Zaslovsky

Brownie
Steiman
1911–1931

Marcie
Steiman
1927–

=

Sidney
Smordin
1924–1996

Cherie
Steiman
1933–

=

Julian B.
Smith
1928–

Mara
Steiman
1921–1973

=

Leonid
Skorupsky

Elizabeth
Smordin
1950–

Elaine
Smordin
1952–

Lyle
Smordin
1956–

Constance
Smith
1958–

=

John
Wiggins
1948–

Gary
Smith
1962–

Margarita
Skorupsky
1945–

=

Shmuel
Konkolsky

Graeme
Wiggins
1977–

Laura Elizabeth
Wiggins
1991–

Donald Hart
Wiggins
1993–

Anna
Konkolsky
1973–

Mark
Konkolsky
1975–

Hannah Zelda[2]
Friedman
1856–1926

=

Mendel
Steiman
1846–1924

Robert
Steiman
1873–1954

=

Sarah
Hornstein
1873–1957

Max
Steiman

Arthur Mayor
Steiman
1892–1977

George
Steiman

Sarah
Steiman

Annie
Steiman

Rose
Steiman

Tzipah
Steiman

Carrie
Steiman
1904–

Mary
Steiman

The Finn Family

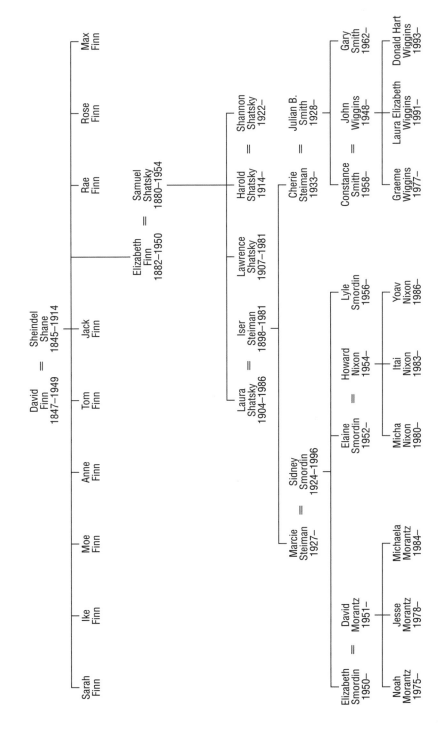

The Shatsky Family

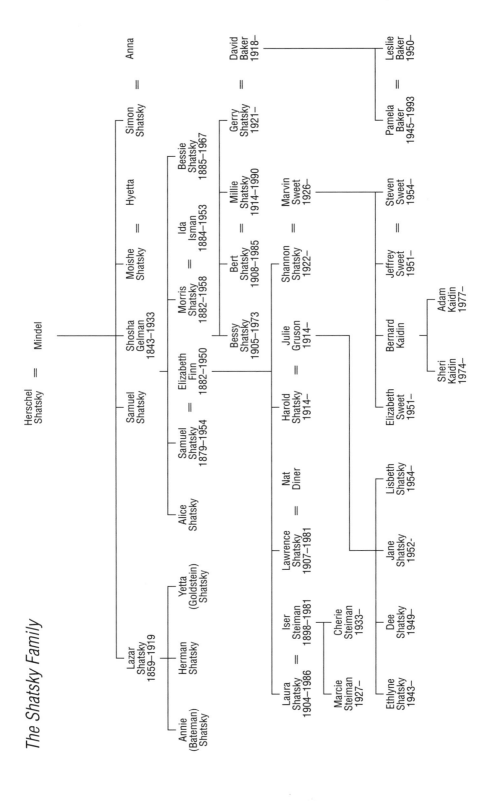

Newcomer

At 12:15 a.m. on November 13, 1933, Dr. Tran being out of town and Dr. Underhill being indisposed (drunk again), Dr. Iser Steiman, with the assistance of nurse Agnes McKie, delivered his second daughter, a 6-lb., 8 oz. sister for six-year-old Marcelyn. Mrs. Steiman (nee Laura Shatsky of Pelly) is resting comfortably at the family home on Third Street.

I was born in the middle of the Great Depression, in the middle of the night, in the middle of a winter storm. My parents, Iser and Laura Steiman, middle-class Jews of East European origin, living in Kamsack, one of the few relatively prosperous towns in the middle of the Canadian prairies, wanted and expected a son. "Peter" was to arrive promptly on November 10, a special birthday present for my mother. And short of inducing labour, my father (who was a general practitioner) attempted to guarantee the event by taking Mother out for a bumpy car ride, walking her up and down stairs and finally, by convincing her to take a large dose of castor oil. All to no avail. A girl already with a mind of her own, I came when I was ready — three days late.

As births in Saskatchewan had to be registered within seven days, I was rather hastily dubbed Shosha Bronya, Yiddish for Sylvia Barbara. Shosha for my mother's grandmother Shatsky, who had just passed away at the age of ninety, and Bronya after my father's youngest sister Brownie, as she was affectionately called, whose sudden death in childbirth in 1931, at the age of twenty, had left my father's family with a profound sense of loss. (It is not in our tradition to name a child after anyone living, lest the angel of death experience confusion in his pick-up orders.) A few weeks later, when I had charmed everyone but my sister Marcie into loving me, my father gave me the name to which I have answered ever since: Cherie.

The house in which I was born was still standing when I went back to look for it fifty-three years after the event. It was being renovated by its most recent owners, a couple in their early twenties, with two small daughters. The young father seemed pleased to let me wander about. The living room, which had remained so large in my memory, now seemed small and cramped. Looking about, I couldn't, for the life of me, figure out how Mother had managed to squeeze in her baby grand piano, overstuffed sofa, big wing chair, coffee table, end tables, bookcases, radio, gramophone console, lamps and of course, that corner curio cabinet on whose open shelves sat untouchable objects of particular fascination for a small girl. I especially recall sitting for hours imagining the life of one china figurine — a flamenco dancer with flashing dark eyes and flaring red skirt, her exquisite little fingers grasping tiny castanets. I've still only to close my eyes to hear the staccato of her shiny black shoes.

My mother, like her mother and all her aunts before her, was the sort of housekeeper whose ambition seemed to be to deny all signs of human habitation. Beds were made early in the day. No signs of life were allowed. No crumbs on or under the table, no stray coffee cups, letters or magazines. A place for everything and everything in its place. If you were reading a book and didn't take it with you when you went to answer the call of nature, it would be gone when you returned. Mother would have swept it up and put it back on the shelf, your place lost. When you railed against this, she would answer that a place in a book could never be lost, it was always there. This was all part of the lifetime war she waged on clutter — everywhere except in my father's library, which was off limits, even to her.

Our dining room was filled with what to me was a massive, dark, English-style carved table, with sideboard and twelve matching chairs. When Mother entertained, all the silver had to be polished beyond perfection, her good linen starched and pressed just so and her children dressed like little angels and on their very best behaviour. The only exception to this was in the early fall when she'd call a corn-eating contest. Then it was rough and tumble all the way. We would sit with big bibs around our necks as huge platters emerged from the kitchen, piled high with steaming cobs of sweet young corn picked that very day, to be followed by pots of melted farm-fresh butter in which to dip them. My mother, always champion of the ladies' team, could eat at least twelve big ones. After the last cob was stripped of its golden harvest, guests would disappear into the kitchen in search of a quick glass of Eno Fruit Salts — just to be on the safe side.

Even in the last six months of her life, though suffering from heart failure, Mother remained indomitable. She dressed fastidiously every morning, if only to sit on the patio enjoying her garden. Indeed, a week before she died, she insisted my sister Marcie take her by wheelchair to see the world's fair, Expo '86 in downtown Vancouver, for eight hours. Her life force was palpable to the very end, so much so that at her funeral a friend came up to me and said, "Your mother has taught us all how to die." But I am getting ahead of my story.

When I came back from Kamsack that same summer of 1986, I brought Mother photographs of our old house and of the town and told her about the changes. And about how some things never change. She smiled when she heard that not only was the bedroom where Marcie and I had slept occupied again by two little girls but, wonder of wonders, that the wallpaper on its ceiling was the very same she herself had put up before I was born. That the last thing these new children, young enough to be her great-granddaughters, would see before falling asleep was our "sky" of silver stars. And like Marcie and me, they would wake up to walk the same half-block to school. The difference was that the sidewalk was now made of cement, not wood planks. No danger of them ever dropping a nickel through the cracks between the boards. No prospect of ever finding one either.

Of course, Kamsack Elementary is no longer the traditional little red schoolhouse of Dick and Jane, but a modern construction with no character whatsoever. Mother took this in without comment. However, when I showed her pictures of the new and very modern Kamsack Union Hospital (and adjacent retirement village) that had replaced Father's King Edward Hospital, she remarked with a certain finality, "Your father did a lot for that town. But it's still a one-horse town and always will be." (My mother was never one to mince words.) I couldn't argue. In fact, what I actually knew about this "one-horse town" that had once been my home, was not much. At fifty-three, however, I was finally at an age where I was interested in finding out.

The town of Kamsack, whose name was derived from the Saulteaux Indian word for "big," is situated at the point where Dead Horse Creek (subsequently renamed Kamsack Creek by the European townsfolk) meets the Assiniboine River and borders two Indian Reserves, the Coté and the Keesekoose. It was at this spot in 1883 that three early pioneers, Moriarty, Scott and Mowat, stopped their Red River carts, pitched their tents and began to homestead. They had correctly judged this land fertile and the climate excellent for growing wheat. One afternoon, a hefty-looking Indian walked into their camp. "What's yer name?" one of the new settlers asked, hoping to get him to work for them. "Kamsack," was his reply. "Sounds like a good name for a town," John Moriarty is alleged to have observed. Certainly, it must have stuck in his mind because a few years later, when the log cabin he'd built became the area's first post office, Moriarty painted "KAMSACK" on an old board and nailed it over his door.

Then in 1901, the Canadian Northern Railway decided to include Kamsack on its main line. It was the custom at this time to set up railway stations every eight to ten miles, so that a settler with his team and wagon could make the round trip from his farm in one day without too much trouble. As a result, a seemingly endless series of thriving villages and towns, each with its own post office, stores and grain elevators, sprang up across the prairies, adding names like Togo, Runnymede, Coté and Veregin to the Canadian map. Suitable "divisional points," stations approximately 150 miles apart with a good water supply for steam engines, had also to be designated. Kamsack, on the banks of the Assiniboine, was obviously ideal. The result was Boom Town. Since it was the "end of the run," many men who worked the trains built homes there and the CNR became Kamsack's biggest employer. On weekends as many as two hundred boxcars filled with livestock would arrive from Alberta, all requiring feed and water.

And with the train came more settlers. A frontier town like Kamsack attracted every kind of people. The British settlers, who began to arrive in the 1880s, were the dominant group politically. And with them came the manners and customs of Victorian England. Indeed, although they worked as hard as anyone else during the week, it was not uncommon to see their Sunday dinner tables covered with white linen tablecloths and set with complete dinner services, including bread and butter plates and serviettes — even on barely developed homesteads. In town, where their husbands had jobs in the professions, the bank, the post office, on the railway, or even as clerks, some of the British women wore hats and gloves and went forth with calling cards for afternoon tea and bridge.

The Ukrainians and Doukhobors, who arrived at the turn of the century, had been among the poorest peasants in Russia and came with neither money nor education. They lived in sod huts until they could build houses, often worked poor soil until they could buy better and suffered the bigotry of their British neighbours, who called them "dirty Galicians" or "hunkies." When a Doukhobor man went home and bled to death after having his tonsils removed, a local English doctor was overheard to dismiss his death with the comment, "One less dirty Douk."

This, of course, was an era not generally noted for racial tolerance and those who suffered most because of this were Canada's First Nations people, who were denied not only their rights as citizens, but their humanity as well. Native Indians from the Reserves outside Kamsack generally came into town on Saturdays to shop and drink. From the viewpoint of many of the locals, the entertainment highlight of each week was the sight of drunken "squaws," as they were commonly called, fighting each other in the middle of Main Street. It was all over at 9:00 p.m. when the curfew came into effect: skirts down, bodies collected, every Indian, sober or otherwise, had to be out of town or else be locked up in the local jail for the night.

Late one stormy winter afternoon in 1928, right after my father, who had just moved his medical practice to Kamsack, was returning from a routine call, he noticed a human form in a snow drift. He asked the sleigh driver to stop.

"Dr. Steiman," he reasoned, "it's just another drunk Indian. Let him freeze."

Father ignored him and got down from the sleigh. In his bulky buffalo coat he sank immediately into snow up to his knees, but he made his way awkwardly to the body to discover it was a young boy.

"He's not drunk," my father called out. "He's fallen asleep from exhaustion. Help me drag him onto the sleigh."

The driver peered at the young Indian. "He's run away from the Mission. We can drop him off there on our way back."

Without comment Father wrapped the boy up in blankets. Soon he began to stir.

"What are you doing out here in this weather?" my father asked.

"Goin' home," the boy mumbled, teeth chattering.

"Where's that?"

"Coté Reserve."

"Turn around, Joe. We're driving him home. I don't believe in taking children away from their parents and converting them." My father would never forget that the Tsar did that for years to the Jews in Russia.

The early Jewish settlers in Kamsack, as elsewhere on the Prairies, were traditionally shopkeepers, itinerant traders, horse dealers, hotel keepers, as well as professional men — doctors, dentists, lawyers. A few families took up farming. The Halters and Kezners bought and sold cattle, horses, hides and furs. The Brounstein brothers started a dairy service from a barn on First Street and supplied milk to about half the town until 1946.

By 1928, Kamsack's population of almost 2,000 included about twenty Jewish families, a number that would double within the decade. Strolling down Main Street in the mid-thirties, you would pass Swartzman's General Store, Kushner's Meat Market, Avrin's Dry Goods and Tailor Shop, Laimon's O.K. Confectionery, Olfman's Meats, Bay's Hardware and Furniture, Blankstein's Jewellery and Rubin's Clothing, Shoes and Boots, as well as the offices of Iser Steiman, physician and surgeon, Archie Rabinovitch, dentist, and Bernard Isman, barrister and solicitor. Finally, you'd reach the King George Hotel (run by Charlie Isman), where you might avail yourself of a drink or two. On high holidays, the tiny synagogue on Fourth Street, with Rabbi Olin officiating, would be filled to bursting.

If the sum of my knowledge about the town in which I had been born and raised was sketchy, so too my grasp of my family's history. Certainly I knew that I was a dues-paid member of an extended collection of people, united by blood, religion and abiding sentiment, who were volatile, often accomplished, sometimes inspiring, occasionally eccentric and to me at least, endlessly fascinating. For example, my father had come to Canada from Russia by himself in 1912 when he was only fourteen-years-old. He had to work hard to earn his board and keep, to learn English, to put himself through high school and then through medical school at the University of Manitoba. In Russia, he and his family had suffered the indignities of second, possibly even third-class citizenship, prisoners within the Pale of Settlement, that portion of the Russian Empire within which ninety-five per cent of all Jews had been confined by edicts of the Tsars from 1772 until 1917, restricted in education and employment opportunities. But he had read the Russian translations of American writer James Fenimore Cooper, especially *The Last of the Mohicans*, and had fallen in love with their new world vision of space and freedom. If the western plains to which he arrived bore little resemblance to the American frontier in Cooper's fiction, the fight between right and wrong, good and evil, still remained, and Father was a fighter. No one was going to push Iser Steiman around or run him out of town.

Iser, who was thirty-five when I was born, had set up practice in Kamsack in 1928, after a number of frustrating years of trying his very best to attend properly to patient needs without hospital facilities in the villages of Benito, Manitoba and Pelly, Saskatchewan (the latter a thirty-mile drive to the north of Kamsack over rough, often impassable roads). And although Kamsack desperately needed a second doctor, he initially found himself pitted against the town's Anglo establishment and their long-time resident physician and surgeon, Charles Tran. A total autocrat, treating only those patients he wanted to, when he wanted to, Tran owned the local hospital, had been town mayor four times and, in effect, ran the place. He wasn't about to have anyone challenging his authority and neither were his local supporters. Rumour had it that over the years they had driven out three other doctors who had attempted to do so.

Father, however, had some distinct advantages of his own. He had boundless energy. He could speak English, Russian, German and Ukrainian. But most of all, he had a talent for humanity. He loved the land and felt at home with the people who worked it. In consequence, it was not long before he became enormously popular, successful and respected. By the end of 1932, with the support of a majority on the town council (which by this time represented interests beyond the congregations of the local United and Anglican Churches), he was able to open his own government-approved hospital at the corner of Second Street and Fifth Avenue, rather grandly naming it the King Edward (not to be confused with the King George, which was the local hotel and beer parlour).

My mother, Laura Shatsky, was only twenty when she met Iser Steiman soon after he had established his practice in Pelly. At five-foot-three inches, with rich brown hair and dark, mischievous eyes, Laura was the eldest of the four Shatsky children. She and her two brothers, Lawrence and Harold, and sister Shannon had all been born in Pelly, where her father and her uncle operated a small general store when they were not trading in horses, cattle and farm produce. Always gutsy, at twelve Mother decided that she had had enough of riding bareback to neighbouring farms and so stole her father's car to teach herself to drive. She was also very bright and might well have had a professional career had she been born a generation later. My grandfather simply didn't believe in sending his daughters to university (something Mother always regretted). He, however, did send her to Winnipeg to complete high school. As a young woman, she dressed in the latest flapper fashion, knew how to dance the Charleston and the Black Bottom, and played the piano well enough to be in demand as an accompanist for the silent movies which were shown at the Pelly town hall to packed audiences. She was also a whiz at bridge and crossword puzzles. What is more, she could change a flat tire in jig time.

It was inevitable that Father, a young and eligible Jewish doctor, would be invited to the Shatskys' for Sabbath dinner. It was equally inevitable that he would be captivated by Laura and intrigued by her mother Elizabeth's condition, yet undiagnosed. (Later he would discover it to be amyotrophic lateral sclerosis, or Lou Gehrig's disease, a slow wasting of the muscles.) But Grandmother Elizabeth was a beautiful person, gentle and kind, a spotless housekeeper and a fine cook and baker. Many years later, Father told me that one of his considerations in deciding to ask my mother to marry him was his conviction that she would take after her mother, and she did. At a time when a person could die from an infected scratch, dirt was Father's prime enemy in his campaign to raise the level of public health in Saskatchewan. After they were married, Mother often went on calls with him to assist in minor surgeries, or mixed prescription powders and salves, rolled bandages, gave inoculations, whatever was necessary.

Sitting on the patio with me that last summer of her life, my mother told me about one of their many adventures. It was early one New Year's Eve, when my father received an emergency telephone call from a remote farm. It was twenty degrees below zero and he was reluctant to go.

"Is it really an emergency?" he asked.

"Yes, yes. My wife — there's something the matter with the way the baby's coming."

"Are the roads passable by car?"

"Yes, yes. Come quick!"

Father got into his felt-lined winter boots, his buffalo coat, his fur hat and gloves. Mother insisted she go along, despite the fact that I was only seven-weeks-old, as he was sure to need help. She, too, bundled up like an Eskimo. The road was treacherous, snow everywhere. And miles from nowhere their Model-A Ford got stuck in a ditch. Father got out his shovel and started to dig. He pushed. They both pushed. A vast white emptiness surrounded them. Brave-faced, they assessed the odds of freezing to death if they stayed with the car, or freezing to death if they started walking. Each silently worried about what would happen to their daughters without them.

Suddenly out of nowhere, they heard a Russian song and wild laughter. For a moment, they thought their minds had gone. Then Father yelled out to them in English.

In the clear cold air he heard a voice in Russian, "It's the police. Keep going."

Father ran in their direction, laughing and calling out in Russian, "It's not the police, it's the doctor. Come and help me!"

In a few minutes, the sleigh full of carousing merrymakers had pushed the car back onto the road.

The result was that the Kamsack district's New Year's baby arrived a few seconds after midnight, albeit feet first, and the grateful farmer paid Father in chickens, eggs and butter.

This was 1934.

Although money was in short supply everywhere, the effects of the world-wide depression, which had struck in 1929, had been slow in reaching Kamsack. Grain was still being shipped through to the newly-built, northern port of Churchill, Manitoba, on Hudson Bay. A local flour mill had opened and was working twenty-four hours a day. Although unemployment had become severe enough to prompt the town into a cost-sharing agreement with the province to create jobs gravelling the streets, food was plentiful and cheap. Although the yield went down by half the average of the 1920s, there was never a crop failure in the Kamsack district. Indeed, in 1933, over thirty thousand pounds of vegetables were sent from our area to drought-stricken towns like Harris, in the dust bowl south-west of Saskatoon. Father's patients, unable to sell their produce for money, more often than not paid him for his services in chickens, eggs, butter, beef, or wood for the furnace.

In many ways, 1933, the year of my birth, had been a watershed in world affairs. In the United States of America, Roosevelt had been sworn in as President, thus ushering in the New Deal. In Germany, Hitler had been named Chancellor, thus condemning the first of millions of European Jews to concentration camps. In Canada, the socialist Cooperative Commonwealth Federation issued its Regina Manifesto, proclaiming the imminence of a secular "New Jerusalem." And I was introduced into the world of a rather older Jerusalem, that of my family, three families actually.

My mother's people, the Shatskys and Finns, had arrived in Canada in 1882, with the first Jewish immigrants from Lithuania and Poland, then part of the Russian empire. Of my father's people, Russian Jews from Latvia, Robert and Sarah Steiman were the first of a family that would arrive in fits and starts over what was almost a century, between 1899 and 1991. By 1905 Robert's parents, my great-grandparents Mendel and Hannah Zelda, arrived with their three sons and five daughters. And what a family I was to discover when I began to piece their stories (and mine) together — immigrant Jews, made bold by their desperation, who found their way to the Canadian West where they scrambled, scrounged and sometimes scoundrelled their living.

The Finn Family Photograph

The first members of my mother's family to immigrate to North America were her grandfather and grandmother, David and Sheindel Finn, and their five children, Annie, Sarah, Rae, Ike and Moe, who arrived in Winnipeg, Manitoba, in June of 1882, part of a second contingent of Russian Jews to immigrate to the Canadian West. Their sixth child, Elizabeth (my mother's mother), was born in the filthy old immigration shed on Fonseca Street shortly after their arrival.

Great-grandfather Finn had been born in Vilna in 1845. Although this historic capital of Lithuania had been incorporated into the Russian Empire in 1795, fifty years later it was still a great centre of Jewish learning and religion. Conditions for its Jewish residents ("citizens" would be a misnomer), however, were about to enter an extended period of general deterioration. Additional restrictions within the Pale of Settlement meant that, with rare exceptions, Russian law forbade Jews to engage in an entire range of professions, businesses and trades and increasingly to own or work farmland. What is more, they were denied the right to travel outside the Pale without special permission. Even more onerous were the special laws enacted in 1827 to impose military service on the Jews.

When Nicholas I resolved to compel the Jews to assimilate, his first step was to enforce a quota of boys and young men from the ages of twelve to eighteen to serve in the army for twenty-five years. He believed there was nothing like army life to squeeze the Jewishness out of a Jew. However, certain categories of Jews were exempted from military duty and were required to pay one thousand rubles "recruiting money." A general law providing that a regular recruit could offer a substitute was extended to the Jews with the proviso that the volunteer must also be a Jew.

This policy failed. Instead of promoting assimilation, it unified the Russian Jews as never before and efforts to avoid the draft increased. My Great-grandfather Shmuel Shatsky, a shoemaker, managed to survive twenty-five years in the army with his Judaism intact.

As general conditions worsened for the Tsarist regime, Jews were relegated to their historical role as scapegoats. Political, economic, or social programs were insufficient to still the revolutionary anger of the Russian masses, so pogroms were often offered instead. These were officially sanctioned attacks, which allowed, indeed encouraged, local Russian anti-Semites to pillage, rape and kill their Jewish neighbours. And, as conditions in Russia became worse, pogroms became more frequent. Thus did poverty and terror become an integral part of Jewish life throughout Eastern Europe. Then the assassination of Tsar Alexander II in 1881, in which a Jew was involved, provided the malevolent, Jew-hating, Russian Minister of the Interior, Count Nikolay Pavlovich Ignatyev (Ignatieff), an excuse to drive Jewish families from their *shtetls* (the small towns and villages they had lived in for generations) through a series of the most brutal pogroms to date in more than two hundred cities and towns, including Kiev, Odessa and Warsaw. Survivors of these attacks told of pregnant women sliced open, of young girls raped and butchered, of babies torn to pieces and tossed into the streets in front of their parents, of children being thrown into wells and drowned in rivers, of homes and shops stripped of their every valuable possession, of whole villages put to the torch and of men being tossed alive into the flames. Although it is probably impossible to describe the horror each Russian Jew held in his or her heart when contemplating a future life within the Pale, it is certain that the pogroms initiated by Ignatyev and his disgusting ilk resulted in the virtual flood of Jewish immigrants from Russia who would seek new lives in America, where it was among other things rumoured that the streets were paved with gold. Some, whose sense of direction was less than perfect, would find their way to Canada.

Great-grandfather Finn had grown up in the winding narrow streets and darkened alleys that honeycombed the Jewish quarter at the foot of Castle Hill, in Vilna's old city. He would later become a butcher by trade and work in a shop (an open stall actually) on Jatkova (Meat Market) Street. As a boy, he attended one of the quarter's many religious schools, but for how long I was unable to discover. I do know that as a man, he went to synagogue regularly, observed all the Orthodox Jewish rituals and lived by the Book. Probably his marriage to Sheindel Shane was an arranged one, but there is no document or memory left to inform us as to the details.

What we do know is that David and Sheindel were in their thirties and had five children when Alexander II was assassinated in March 1881. News of the Ignatyev-sponsored pogroms in the south spread quickly. Thousands of Jews spontaneously fled the Pale, the Finns among them. Thus began a migration comparable in modern Jewish history only to the flight from the Spanish Inquisition in the fifteenth century. With typical Tsarist perversity, the Russian government made it difficult for Jews to get passports, yet tolerated illegal border crossings. I do not know exactly how Great-grandfather got his family out of Russia, but it seems most likely that they proceeded by train to some village near the Prussian border, where someone, quite possibly another Jew, smuggled them across the German border in a hay wagon for a "mere" three rubles a head. Once in Eydtkuffnen, or some other German town, they probably would have made their way to Hamburg, where a Jewish committee to support Russian immigrants had been set up to provide passage to Liverpool.

European and American Jews had reacted to the plight of their Russian co-religionists by setting up immigrant relief and resettlement organizations. On February 2, 1882, for example, prominent British Jews met at London's Mansion House with Sir Alexander Galt, Canada's High Commissioner to Great Britain and the London representative of the Canadian Pacific Railway, who agreed to make land and work available in Canada for displaced Russian Jews. Huge sums of money were raised to facilitate the exodus and by mid-June about seven thousand Russian Jews had arrived in the United States and Canada. Montreal's Jewish community hastily set up a relief committee to prepare for the arrival of the first immigrants. Great-grandfather Finn and his family were among them. A ticket to Canada cost about sixty to seventy rubles, the equivalent of thirty to thirty-five dollars. Not in a lifetime could a poor man like David Finn, who probably never earned more than one ruble or one ruble and fifty kopecks a day, have ever afforded the fare for his entire family.

One thing I do know for certain is that the Finn family had never been on a ship before and had no idea of what was in store for them. The seven of them were herded up the gangplank along with hundreds of others, onto a deck with blistering paint and rusty railings, through a hatchway and down two flights of steep, slippery, metal stairs, everyone pushing and struggling to arrive first to gain such advantage as they might. But all for naught. Steerage was steerage: dark and stifling, three tiers of hard bunks bolted to the decks above and below, row upon row between the bulkheads, under the water line, over the engines. The noise was deafening, the vibrations endless. The Finn family was fortunate enough to find bunks together and settled down as best they could in conditions unfit for cattle. Initially, they worried that the food ladled from the huge kettles into their dinner pails was not kosher and would not eat it. A day later, in the sea's increasing roll, food became the least of their considerations. Everyone was desperately ill. Babies vomited their mother's milk. As the days and nights passed into weeks, the stench and accumulated filth became intolerable, the washrooms indescribably foul. There was no escape, except for the fearful deck of a ship tossing wildly in the Atlantic Ocean. Great-grandfather had to drag Sheindel, now eight months pregnant, up to get the air. He was afraid she would die otherwise. Indeed, he dragged the children up as well, and those old enough to remember would never forget the experience. As sick as they were, no one dared to disobey him.

When the ship finally reached Halifax, the family, weak and reeling, stumbled, in an hallucinatory stupor, down the gangplank, the buildings along the dock swimming before their eyes. Herded into an immigration shed, they filed past a doctor. Those immigrants whose health was obviously suspect were marked with chalk for later inspection. An interpreter asked each one a question or two to determine if he or she were mentally fit. A second doctor checked for contagious diseases, venereal and other. A third checked for whatever, and further on, nurses waited at delousing stations.

After the family had survived the poking of their bodies and the prying into their private parts, their papers were duly processed and they were allowed to stagger on to the next line-up, where at last they were fed. Eventually the family, along with about two hundred other immigrants destined for Winnipeg, was loaded into colonist cars on a westbound Intercolonial Railway train. After steerage, this hard-class transportation must have felt like the Orient Express. And so began yet another journey without apparent end, this time across a seemingly limitless land: Nova Scotia, New Brunswick, northern Maine, the Eastern Townships of Quebec and at last, Montreal. Here they were met by the Young Men's Hebrew Benevolent Society, which provided them with meals they could in conscience eat, as well as with any required medical aid, before sending them on their way across Ontario to Toronto and eventually to Sarnia. There was no completed Canadian railway north beyond this point. The SS Ontario would ferry them the several days across Lakes Huron and Superior (the latter, the world's largest fresh water sea) to Duluth, Minnesota. Fortunately, because the weather was clear and their ship a laker and relatively small, their steerage accommodation proved no great hardship as they were able to spend the pleasant spring days on deck. The Northern Pacific Railway would carry them over the last long lap across Minnesota, across the Manitoba border at Emerson and on to Winnipeg and the welcome of that city's pioneer Jewish community.

The first Jews to settle permanently in Winnipeg had come from England, Germany and the United States in 1878. They were mostly merchants of modest means and adherents of the Reform branch of Judaism. English-speaking and well-integrated into the larger, mainly British Canadian society, they had established themselves around Logan and Main Streets, then the centre of Winnipeg's business district. By the time the Finns arrived in 1882, there were in fact thirty-eight such families to give the newcomers assistance.

The Federal Immigration Branch had provided the local Jewish community a big, old, filthy shed near the Red River, on Fonseca Street West, in which to house the immigrants temporarily. But there had been little time to provide the amenities necessary to accommodate the numbers who arrived. Nevertheless, David and Sheindel Finn, their five children and the other one hundred and ninety-odd Jewish immigrants were each grateful for that first kosher dinner of half a potato and a bowl of watery porridge sweetened with dark syrup.

Scarcely had they finished this feast when a representative from the firm Jarvis and Berridge offered the men immediate work at twenty-five cents an hour unloading two rafts of lumber which had just been brought up from Emerson on the SS Omega. David Finn and the others promptly lined up to march down to the Red River, where they unloaded the lumber all night, happy to be working and earning their first Canadian money after such a long and trying journey. They worked until 6 a.m., then returned to the Immigration shed to sleep on the floor. It was here, a few days later, that Sheindel Finn gave birth to the girl child Elizabeth, who would, fifty-one years later, become my grandmother.

Now with a wife and six children to provide for, David Finn took whatever work was available, loading gravel in the pits of the Manitoba and Southwestern Colonization Railway, digging ditches, excavating basements. That summer, from July to October, he worked for the Canadian Pacific Railway, splitting ties at Whitemouth, Manitoba, grading and ballasting the rail line and laying the track to Medicine Hat. The Railway was speeding its way west to British Columbia and the pay was a relatively decent two dollars to two dollars, fifty cents a ten-hour day, plus board and room.

About one hundred and fifty Russian Jews worked on this section of the line, living in CPR construction crew boarding cars, sleeping in the upper section and using the lower as a mess hall. Kosher food was provided and they were excused from working Friday evening to Saturday at sundown so that they could observe the Sabbath. They had brought a Holy Scroll and were permitted the use of a company tent for their weekly services. The first night on the job at Whitemouth, however, about seventy fellow workers attacked them in an anti-Semitic frenzy with stones and clubs, a terrifying reminder of the pogroms they had just escaped. Two weeks later while they were laying track at Rosser Station, Great-grandfather's friend, Kiva Barsky, was hit on the head with an iron bar in another outbreak of racist violence. Fortunately, David Finn was about as strong and tough as they come, and nobody got the best of him in a fight if the odds were anywhere close to even.

Over that first summer, these new Jewish immigrants earned anywhere from three hundred to three hundred and fifty dollars clear, more money than they had ever earned before. And upon returning to Winnipeg, many of them, Great-grandfather included, used this capital to underwrite peddling businesses, or to open small shops. By this time, David had managed to get Sheindel and their children settled in a district of Winnipeg which the gentiles were soon to call "New Jerusalem." Here, in the city's North End, Jews

New Jerusalem, corner of Dufferin and King,
Winnipeg, 1904, courtesy Manitoba Archives

from Poland, the Ukraine and Russia would recreate their *shtetl* lifestyle in this their new land, with modifications of course. They had to speak English to do business outside their own neighbourhood, but at home and in the streets of "New Jerusalem," they spoke Yiddish.

In 1882, Winnipeg was booming, with a population of about twenty thousand and growing fast. There were no sidewalks and the streets were potholed beyond belief in summer, and were a sea of gumbo mud in the spring. But a man willing to work could succeed. Blind luck, however, can never be discounted and as chance would have it, David was peddling fish one day when he met a man who was peddling a cow. After some spirited haggling, David bought it and when it was killed and dressed, he sold the meat at a good profit. So good that he decided to establish a wholesale meat business, calling it David Finn Livestock, a venture that was to continue from the early 1890s until his retirement in 1918 at the age of seventy-three. Somewhere along the way, his name Fayn became Finn, most probably coming through Immigration at Halifax, given the language barrier that would have separated him and the Canadian official processing his papers. On his sixtieth birthday, one of his employees bet him that he could not lift a three-hundred pound side of beef from the back of the delivery wagon and hang it on a loading dock meat hook. He took the challenge and won.

Physically powerful, Great-grandfather also had a reputation for being strong-willed and opinionated. When religious differences arose in the Jewish community between the English and German Jews, who favoured Reform Judaism, and the Russian and Polish Jews, who were Orthodox, he was one of the leaders responsible for building the Rosh Pina Orthodox Synagogue at Martha and Henry Streets in 1893.

As the meat business thrived, he was able to acquire a larger house for the family on Robson Street, with acreage and a barn big enough for the horses and wagons he needed to deliver dressed carcasses to retail butcher shops. Besides, Great-grandmother continued to give birth and they needed the space. Eventually, there were to be ten children (to say nothing of a never-ending stream of visitors) crowding their dinner table. With their growing prosperity, Sheindel bought new furniture. She bought a piano, the younger Finns took music lessons. She bought wallpaper, she redecorated. Amazingly tiny and slender after all those babies, she developed a taste for fine clothes. As soon as the children were old enough or had finished high school, however, they were expected to find work and to make their contribution to the family coffers. Annie and Sarah, for example, went to work in the cigar and cigarette factories; Moe and Tommy into the meat business with their father.

A couple of months after his first grandchild was born, David Finn decided it was time to have the family photograph taken. He had certainly done well since coming to Canada. And his grandchild, Mamie, represented a second generation born in Canada, something he didn't talk about much but felt deeply. There was much excitement when he announced at the Sabbath table that the photographer was coming on Sunday. "You should all be ready by two o'clock sharp," he said. They would be. Including Sarah, her husband Jake and, of course, the baby. Great-grandfather's word was still law. Besides, this was an event.

One can imagine the older girls helping wash and dress the younger children after their lunch on Sunday: Maxie stuffed resentfully into his scratchy sailor suit; Rose (later to be nicknamed Rose-with-the-nose) insisting on wearing her blue velvet trimmed with lace; two-year-old Jack buttoned into a pure white cotton smock, his hair slicked down with a mixture of sugar and water; Baby Mamie, in a long white dress with puffed, drawstringed sleeves and lace bib, a small curl falling over her forehead "just like her mama"; Sarah handing Mamie over to Rae, while she fusses about her

Jake's tie. When the photographer arrives and sets up his tripod, there are a few last-minute adjustments to hair and dresses. Finally, David Finn says, in a loud voice, "Enough already," and a short-lived silence falls over the room. And Sheindel comes down the stairs wearing her black peau-de-soie, with velvet epaulets and bib trimmed with braid.

The photographer proceeds to arrange the group. David he places in the middle of the brocade settee, with Sheindel to his left and Sarah holding Mamie on his right. Then he arranges the rest: Ike, Jake, Moe, Tommy at the back and solid, square-faced Annie standing at the end of the row like a column. Rose sits on the floor upon a velvet cushion and Maxie on an embroidered footstool. The photographer checks to make sure the patriarch's embroidered black velvet *yarmulke* (skullcap) is on absolutely straight, then

The Finn Family, back row left to right: Ike, Jake Barnes, Moe, Annie; centre row: Rae, Sarah holding Mamie, David, Sheindel, Tommy, Elizabeth; front row: Rose, Jack, Maxie, Winnipeg, circa 1894

retreating to his large portrait camera, raises his hand. *"Sha schtill."* Recorded for eternity, it is over in a flash of magnesium powder and potassium chlorate!

The result is a photo-portrait dominated by Great-grandfather Finn's tremendous strength. He sits straight, shoulders braced, one hand on young Jack's arm, restraining him, his eyes stern, unsmiling, looking right past the photographer, thinking perhaps that Sarah's Jake will never be successful, that Annie should be

David Finn on his 100th birthday, with son Jack, Winnipeg, 1947

married soon, that Rae is too much like himself, causing trouble already. And Elizabeth, even more beautiful than Sheindel, is becoming too fond of her cousin Bob Rosenblatt. He will marry her off to young Samuel Shatsky, a good-looking man with ambition, who had come from Poland as a boy. And the sooner the better. The boys, however . . . they'll get along . . . with his help. What he doesn't know is that he will live to be one hundred and two. That on one evening in 1914, his beloved Sheindel will collapse in his arms as she is dressing for a party, and die. That he will marry again only six months later despite his children's disapproval. That he will outlive his second wife and marry yet a third. That he will outlive her as well and will, at the age of ninety-eight, lay new linoleum on the kitchen floor. Or that on his one hundredth birthday, he will see his picture in the Winnipeg Free Press and receive a telegram of congratulations from the King of England.

Sheindel, who has given birth to the entire brood, gazes out, past the photographer in the same direction as David. There is no sign of fatigue or ill temper in her expression. Yet, even at this happy moment with all her children around her, she feels a mother's cold shiver of fear, a sense of doom when she looks at Mamie and Elizabeth. She doesn't know why she feels it, but she is right. Through her genes, Sheindel has passed to them a slowly degenerative muscle disease not then diagnosable. And to young Jack she has passed on her weak heart. She is conscious of her older sons behind her. They are good-looking, amiable and undemanding, more like her, she thinks, but not nearly as ambitious as she and David would like.

Moe, with the weak chin and vague look, will marry a domineering woman and become a second-hand furniture dealer in Vancouver. Maxie, cowering in the corner, will spend his life working as a night dispatcher for a taxi company in Chicago. Tommy, smiling broadly on the far left, will move to Paradise — Los Angeles — open a linoleum store and marry a *shikse* (a gentile). Young Jack will become an insurance salesman and enjoy an extended bachelorhood until over forty. Ike, standing next to Jake, the only one of the men in the picture who is well-dressed, wearing a smartly-cut tweed suit, will spend his life "in haberdashery."

But what of the five daughters? David's great strength was passed on, as is often strangely the case, to "the girls," except perhaps for Elizabeth, who although she inherited his stubbornness, will remain gentle, soft-spoken and uncomplaining. Rae, domineering, stubborn, opinionated, would live well into her nineties. Defiant and daring, she will inevitably clash with David. But what a beauty! With David's blue eyes, she is tall and blond, with fine legs and a good bust. Elizabeth, her foil, has dark hair and eyes, but both have flawless complexions. When they go skating in their stylish costumes, heads turn, boys gather around. David senses trouble and is particularly anxious to marry Rae off, but she's already turned down an offer from Sam Bronfman: "Papa, he is only a drayman and besides, he picks his nose!" Later, during prohibition, Sam will become a millionaire from rum-running and bootlegging. Rae, however, will have no regrets, and years later will still laugh about it: "He may be a millionaire, but he still picks his nose." Instead, she will marry Phillip Brotman, a dapper dandy, a gambling kind of man, whose finances will always be unstable but whose manners were impeccable. Later, David's third daughter, Annie, will marry, and Rose-with-the-nose will fall for a Rothschild — probably the only poor one in existence!

But for now it is a happy day. The photographer folds up his tripod and departs. Tea and cakes are brought out. Rae and Elizabeth take turns at the piano and the boys gather around to sing. David and Sheindel sit on the settee. When she looks up, Sheindel notices David brush away a tear. She puts down her teacup to take his hand in hers.

T H E S C H L E M I E L A N D
T H E S C H L E M A Z E L

To the right of the patriarch in the Finn family photograph sits the eldest daughter. Sarah is wearing a dark dress, with puffed leg-of-mutton sleeves and white lace collar. Her auburn hair is tightly curled, with that one precious lock falling in the centre of her splendidly high forehead. Her face and body are as softly rounded as a wren's. Her head is slightly cocked, as if she were listening to music no one else can hear. Behind her stands her husband, her dashing, handsome Jake, tall, with wavy dark hair and full lips under a handlebar moustache, his bright eyes confident as he looks into the camera.

Sarah and Jake were mad about each other and remained so all their lives. Theirs had been love at first sight. In an age when such things were considered near scandalous, they held hands, even hugged, in public. When she looked at him she practically bubbled with joy. She sat on his knee and called him her prince. He called her "my Sarah, my princess." Mamie, Jake and Sarah's first child, the dear thing on Sarah's knee in the family photograph, might as well have been an orphan for all the attention they gave her. In fact, she was hardly six-months-old when they gave her to Great-grandmother Sheindel to bring up. After all, who would notice another child in the crowded Finn household? So, for the first few years of her life, Mamie called her grandmother "Ma," and her grandfather "Pa," her own parents just incidental, less important to her happiness than her aunts and uncles. But she was loved by everyone, perhaps even more so because of this. As to Jake and Sarah, so grand was their passion, they didn't know Mamie, or anyone else, existed.

Sarah, of course, didn't care that Jake was a prince without a penny to his name. Great-grandfather Finn had more than enough pennies to help them get started, or restarted, which was just as well, because Jake proved to be as unlucky in business as he was lucky in love. Take, for example, his short career as a fisherman. At the time, ice fishing was still done commercially on Lake Winnipeg, which was renowned for its fine white fish. In twenty-below-zero winter weather, men would bundle up, tuck flasks of overproof spirits into their pockets, harness up their horses and drive their sleighs to the lake. There, they would cut holes in the ice, lower their nets and await their fortunes . . . warming themselves as best they could. Normally, they would return to Winnipeg loaded — in more ways than one. Of course Lake Winnipeg was vast and bleak, the wind blowing in from all directions, making twenty-below feel more like forty. Naturally, Great-grandfather Finn had had to arrange for Jake's sleigh and horses. And Jake, for his part, occasionally managed to pull himself away from Sarah long enough to make quite a few good hauls. But on his last trip, just before spring break-up, the ice cracked. Down went sleigh, horses, fish, and Uncle Jake. But the lucky *schlemazel* was pulled free by the other fishermen, saved, so to speak, by a hair on his fashionable handlebar moustache.

While Jake was recovering from his icy encounter with Lake Winnipeg, Great-grandfather married off another daughter, Sarah's younger sister Elizabeth (my grandmother) to Sam Shatsky (my grandfather), another pauper prince perhaps, but one with promise. When Great-grandfather Finn heard that a small hotel in Grenfell, a village half-way between the present Manitoba-Saskatchewan border and Regina, was up for sale, he bought it for his two sons-in-law to manage. An ideal solution it was not. From the start Sam and Jake did not get along. "I cannot work with a *schlemiel* or with a *schlemazel*," Sam told his father-in-law, "and Jake is both."

A *schlemiel* is someone who cannot seem to do anything right and a *schlemazel* is someone who is habitually unlucky. When a *schlemiel* knocks over a bowl of chicken soup, it lands on the *schlemazel*. And it was becoming apparent to the entire family that Sam's opinion of Jake was too true for everyone's financial comfort. But by now Jake and Sarah had two more children, a boy and girl, and had taken back, or been given back, Mamie. As they could not be left to their own devices, or so it was thought, it was imperative to find something for Jake, and as *mazel* (good luck) would have it, an opportunity arose in Fort William (now Thunder Bay), Ontario, at the head of Lake Superior and a good long way from Winnipeg. This time, it was a hole-in-the-wall butcher shop on Simpson Street.

But cutting and selling meat is not as simple as it sounds. Jake, who didn't know the hind end of a cow from a barn door, or a knife from a scale, and whose only experience with meat was eating whatever parts, boiled, fried, stewed, or roasted were set before him, was about to learn the complexities of running a butcher shop. Each part of the unfortunate animal sells at a different price. Then there are the ups and downs of a temperamental scale. Then there are pounds and ounces and fractions thereof to contend with, as well as the higher mathematics involved in keeping accounts. Not to mention dealing with customers. Every housewife wants the best, the tenderest, and the tastiest for the least amount of money. And a good housewife knows her meat.

God knows, Jake was no great shakes as a salesman, but there were a couple of factors in his favour: he was excruciatingly clean and exceedingly handsome. In addition, because he never ceased being crazily in love with his dear, dear Sarah, he always had a ready smile for all the women who entered his shop, whether they were young or old, pretty or ugly. If a customer asked him if the meat he was showing her was good, he'd reply in all seriousness, "It's so good, I'd eat it myself if I didn't need the money."

A butcher shop, however, is a mighty perilous place for a maladroit, disaster-prone man and it was not long before Jake added a finger to Mrs. Greenberg's, or was it Mrs. McIvor's, ground round. Again with the loving care of Sarah, he recovered. And together, they were able to eke out a precarious living until their children were old enough to leave home.

It was only then that Jake and Sarah made their exodus to Paradise. For many Canadian Jews (and apparently for nearly everybody else), Paradise was California in general, and Los Angeles in particular. Why be a poor *schlemazel* in the cold and snow in Fort William, where you were lucky to get sixty days a year without frost, when you could be a poor *schlemazel* in Paradise? Poverty was a bitter pill in any case, but more easily swallowed with juice from oranges grown in your own backyard. And if you didn't have furs on your back or diamonds on your fingers, so what? Everyone knew the best things in life were free! Hadn't Sarah's brother, Tommy, found prosperity in L.A. even if he had married a gentile, a *shikse*? So off they went, Jake and Sarah, to find a nest just big enough for two in one of the poorer sections of Los Angeles, where they lived on love and welfare and a little help from their children. When the two of them finally became ill and infirm, they stayed together, sharing each other's suffering as they had shared their lives and love for over sixty years. They died within a very short time of each other, lucky in love to the end.

LADY BALTIMORE
CAKE

It is raining. Pouring, in fact. A typical November day in Vancouver. Sitting at my kitchen table, I am idly turning the pages of an old family cookbook, wondering whether to spend the afternoon baking or writing, when a recipe catches my eye.

My Grandmother Elizabeth was famous for her Lady Baltimore cake: a delicately-flavoured, fine-textured creation with a rich icing, more suited for a tea in an elegant English drawing room than her small country sitting room in the Saskatchewan village of Pelly, population 257. But then Grandmother Elizabeth, as I recall her, a slim, fragile, fine-featured, ivory-complexioned, soft-spoken, white-haired woman, was equally out of place among the slop pails, hand pumps, woodpiles and hen houses. Yet, to my knowledge, she never put on airs or complained of the life she was to play out with Grandpa Sam against this rustic backdrop.

The Shatsky town property in Pelly (Grandpa Sam owned a small farm which was run by a tenant a few miles down the Kamsack Road) consisted of a small clapboard house with a wide, screened-in veranda and a large combination barn, hen house and garage on a half acre, bordered on one side by a row of silver poplars that formed a windscreen and on the other by a carragana hedge. Its several garden plots were devoted to vegetables, raspberry bushes and masses of sweet william, delphiniums, gladioli, phlox, daisies, sweet peas, sunflowers, peonies, prize-winning lilacs and more. In midsummer, the air around their house was so golden, so balmy and sweet that I was sure winter would never dare to enter so enchanted a place. Yet come December, as a little girl, I would flop down into the deep snow and wave my arms, totally oblivious that I was making short, stubby angels over the very spot where, not many months before, daisies had nodded in the sun.

When Grandmother Elizabeth baked, she used only the freshest eggs, and often I would be dispatched to gather them. I would start out boldly, but when I reached the hen house a

Samuel and Elizabeth Shatsky, Winnipeg, 1903

little shiver of fear would run down my back. First I would peer through the dirty, fly-specked windows. Then, slowly and carefully, I would open the creaky wooden door, look into the darkness beyond, pungent with the warm smell of hay and chicken manure. I would listen to the gentle clucking of the nervous hens in their boxes and the soft cooing of the brown and white tumbler pigeons in the rafters. Conscious of a hundred beady eyes upon me watching my every move, I would step inside and softly close the door, looking for Henny Penny, my favourite Rhode Island Red. Suddenly, my worst fear would be realized — a rooster would swoop down at me, squawking and flapping, sending up a cloud of spangled dust glittering with insects and threads of golden straw caught in the shafts of sunlight that had managed to filter through the dusty windowpanes. In a second, I would be back outside, my heart beating as if it would burst. Plucking up my courage, I would venture in again, moving slowly toward the nesting hens. Acknowledging their squawks of protest with my own soft noises, I would push my hand under their fat, feathered bottoms to draw out the warm brown eggs.

Back in Grandmother Elizabeth's kitchen, the wood-burning McClary range would have reached the required temperature, as Grandmother set out milk and flour, fresh butter, sugar, whisks, beaters, bowls and pans. All was ready for the cake-making ritual. I would sit down on the bench with a glass of milk and a cookie, to watch and wait until I was handed an empty mixing bowl to lick clean. When the cakes were popped into the oven, Grandmother would start on cookies or pies. "I might as well," she invariably would say, "the oven is just right." And from an unbleached cotton bag of cottage cheese hung above the sink, drops of milky liquid would plop irregularly into a dish below, punctuating the afternoon like commas.

I did not know Grandmother Elizabeth when she was a young woman. When I was eight she was fifty-nine. She would appear in the morning at her bedroom door fully-dressed, wearing a fresh cotton house dress buttoned down the front, and a small white apron tied around her waist, her grey hair slightly blue with rinse, tightly curled over her ears. It seems amazing to me now, but I never heard her raise her voice. She seemed to have endless patience, sitting at the long kitchen table playing cards — Fish or War — with me. I was aware that she did not have much strength and suffered from "spells" in which she could not catch her breath. I now know that she was suffering from both Lou Gehrig's disease and bulbar palsy. When I was a little girl, however, I was told that she had never really recovered from being badly burned in a fire.

After the breakdown of Grandpa's partnership with Great-uncle Jake in the hotel business, Great-grandfather Finn had set Grandpa and Grandma Shatsky up in a little general store in Benito, across the Manitoba border from Pelly. Both Grandpa and Grandma were in the store when some kerosene gas exploded and Grandma was instantly engulfed in flames. She instinctively covered her face with her arms. Grandfather, who was also burned, hauled her out of the flaming store and plunged her into a barrel of rainwater that stood outside the door. The townsfolk bundled both of them in blankets, loaded them onto a railway handcar and hand-pumped them the fifteen miles north to Swan River and the closest doctor. Grandmother's beautiful face was saved at the cost of her arms, which were severely scarred. The combs she had been wearing in her hair had melted in the intense heat and had dripped down her neck, leaving a series of droplet scars down her back which I remember touching and even counting when she was having a bath and called me in to give her back a "good scrubbing."

Whenever I visited Pelly, I slept with Grandma in the big bed in her room at the end of the hall near the veranda. Otherwise, she slept alone. "Why do you sleep here and Grandpa there?" I asked one night, snuggling next to her. "Grandpa snores too loud," she said. And he did, but now I know that Grandma and Grandpa slept apart because after six pregnancies and the loss of two babies, Grandma did not want to be bothered by him, like that, any more. So he slept in his own room down the hall.

Because Grandma Elizabeth was fragile and required help with the household chores, there was always a live-in, farm-fresh girl to do the cleaning, the carrying, the collecting of chamber pots, the tending of the kitchen garden and the myriad other jobs that had to be done in a country home in the 1930s. The girls were usually not more than sixteen and had only a few years of rural elementary education. Their real education was just about to begin. Grandmother taught them how to make a bed properly, how to serve at table, how to scrub and wax a floor, how to make a perfect pie crust and perfect cinnamon buns, how to preserve peaches, put down dill pickles, how to make sauerkraut and corned beef. It was hard work, but the girls became part of the family; they ate with the family, went on outings with the family and travelled wherever the family went.

On Friday nights Mary, the hired girl, would throw a clean white cloth over the table. Then Grandmother Elizabeth would place her grandmother's shiny brass candlesticks in the exact centre of the table. A small glass of wine and a freshly baked *challah* (a braided loaf) she would set directly in front of Grandpa Sam's plate. Next to her perfect, shining brown loaf I put my small, clumsily-braided version. At sundown, we gathered around the table. Grandmother, with a lacy scarf on her head, would strike a match, light the candles and with her eyes closed, sing in her soft voice the *brocha* (prayer), all the while inscribing small circles with her fragile hands, translucent in the candlelight.

Baruch ato adonai
Eloheynu melech haolam
Asher kidshanu bmitzvosav
Vtzivanu lhadlik ner
Shel Shabbos. Amen

"What's that mean?" I asked no one in particular.

"It means," Grandmother Elizabeth answered calmly, "be praised, Lord our God, who has sanctified us by His laws and commanded us to light the Sabbath candles."

But I had already lost interest in what she was saying and was staring transfixed at the glittering glass of red wine that Grandpa Sam was holding up to the candlelight. His fingers were thick and the back of his hands freckled. On his curly reddish hair he wore a small black cap he called a *yarmulke*. He was speaking very fast. All I could catch were the words he said quite clearly and grandly.

"Bo-rey p'-ree ha-ga-fin. Amen."

"What's that mean, Grandpa?"

He took a sip and put the glass down.

"It means," he said, "be praised, Lord our God, King of the Universe, Creator of the fruit of the vine. And now for the *motzi*." He drew the plate with the *challah* closer and once again mumbled or spoke so quickly that I missed everything except:

"Ha-mo-tzi le-chem-min ha-a-retz. Amen."

"What's that mean, Grandpa?"

"It means," he said while tearing off a piece of the *challah*, stuffing it into his mouth and passing the plate along, "it means be praised, Lord our God, King of the Universe, who causes the earth to yield food."

"Oh," I said, chewing on my piece of bread for a second, "well, you forgot to bless my *challah*, Grandpa."

"No I didn't, Cherie," he said, "I'm just about to. But I am not blessing the bread or the wine, I am praising God and thanking him for the food he gives us." And with that, he repeated the whole incantation over my pathetic little *challah* and tore off a piece, chewed it enthusiastically and sent the rest on its way around the table.

It's very strange, I thought as I spooned my chicken soup, that God should be thanked when I knew I had seen and had helped Grandmother make the bread.

But I was soon distracted from these profound questions by Mary setting before Grandpa a whole roasted chicken surrounded by potatoes and carrots. I looked at the chicken, then frowned at Grandpa.

"That's not Henny Penny, is it, Grandpa?"

"Of course not."

"Are you sure?"

"Of course it's not Henny Penny," Grandmother said. "This bird is twice Henny's size."

"Well, if you say so."

"You don't have to worry, Cherie, we'll never eat Henny Penny," Grandpa assured me, as he started to carve the bird.

"Promise?"

"I promise."

"Okay, then can I have a wing?"

Monday was washday, all day. This was the one day of the week when people under four feet tall, if found underfoot, were not looked upon kindly by hired girls or grandmothers. Little people were continually admonished to keep out of the way, to stand aside, and were told repeatedly about Johnny Popoff, who had been told not to, but put his hand too close to the wringer on the Maytag washing machine, which had grabbed his fingers and flattened them. Or little Annie Kolaidachuk, who had been badly scalded when a pail of boiling water had tipped over. It seemed that there was a never-ending supply of washday horror stories, all designed to keep me from helping.

So I would watch as dirty laundry was carefully sorted and separated into piles according to colour and degree of grime. The whites went into the hot soapy water first, then were fed through the wringer. Next, the coloured items went into the same soapy water. And so on. The water was then drained out of the Maytag into pails, carried down the back stairs and thrown somewhere onto something which needed a good sluicing off. The washing machine was then refilled with clean, warm rinse water and the process repeated until all of the laundry lay in a fragrant heap in a big wicker basket. Carrying a pail of wooden clothes pegs, I would follow Mary as she lugged the heavy basket to the four lines strung out between poles near the woodpile. As she threw the great white sheets over the line, I was ready to thrust the wooden pegs into her large, red, rough hands with their stubby fingers and short clean nails. When everything had been hung out on the line in order of size, colour and respectability (unmentionable items were always hung on the middle lines so as to be invisible to passers-by), we would run back into the house to drain the remaining rinse water, clean the machine, pull out the cord and start preparing for lunch, which was really dinner.

Later in the day, afternoon or evening, depending on the weather, we'd go out again with the wicker basket and the clothespeg pail to take the warm, dry clothes off the line. Back in the house, each item was laid upon the table and sprinkled lightly with water from a beer bottle with a spray stopper, then rolled up and put back into the basket, which would then be covered with a clean towel. In the winter, Mary would gather in the frozen sheets and clothes, crack them in half and stumble through the snow towards the basement steps, the arms and legs of Grandfather's long underwear gesticulating wildly from her basket. Then, with numb white hands she would lay them over the wooden clotheshorse near the furnace to dry. Ironing was always scheduled for the next day.

On Tuesday morning, two heavy irons would be put on the back of the stove to heat. After all the morning chores were done and the lunch dishes put away, when Grandpa went to his room for a nap and Grandma, still wearing her little white apron, lay down on the red frieze couch in the living room and put on her glasses to read a detective magazine, Mary would set up the ironing board. Soon the kitchen was filled with the steamy smell of warm clean sheets and shirts.

Grandpa Sam rose very early in the mornings, usually at three or four o'clock. He would have finished all his chores by the time I trudged down the hall in my flowered flannel pyjamas to peek into the kitchen. Invariably, he would be reading yesterday's paper at a small wooden table by the side window that looked out onto a bit of lawn and a hedge of lilac bushes. Seeing me, he would get up to make me a cup of cocoa, then cut a big slice of fresh bread, clamp it in a long-handled wire rack and hold it over the coals of the range to toast it. Munching my toast, I would watch him pop a lump of sugar into his mouth, then sip hot coffee from a saucer, which he held in both of his hands. It was an "old country"

Elizabeth Shatsky, Pelly, Saskatchewan, 1937

custom that was not allowed at Grandmother's table, but one in which he could safely indulge before anyone of consequence was up.

The only time Grandma Elizabeth refused to leave the kitchen was while her Lady Baltimore cake was baking; the oven temperature had to be checked, more wood slipped into the firebox. She fretted over it like a speckled hen over her chicks. Little people were admonished not to slam the door or jump off chairs. "The cake will fall," she said. I wondered — how could a cake fall? I had a vision of it falling, a cake with mountain peaks of white icing on a big white plate, falling gently through the blue sky, through fluffy white clouds, through the open window and landing right before me on the wooden table in Grandmother's kitchen.

"It's done," Grandmother announced, breaking my reverie. Carefully she removed the cake from the oven and placed it on the table before me. Its rich vanilla aroma engulfed me, impressing it forever in my memory!

LADY BALTIMORE CAKE

1 cup butter

1 cup milk

2 cups fine sugar

1 tsp. vanilla extract

3 cups pastry flour

1 tsp. almond extract

3 tsp. baking powder

6 egg whites

1/4 tsp. salt

Preheat oven to 350°. Cream butter and 1 cup of sugar thoroughly. Add extracts. Sift flour, baking powder and salt three times, add to butter mixture alternately with milk. Beat egg whites until foamy, gradually add remaining sugar and beat until stiff. Fold into batter. Bake in two paper-lined 8 inch round pans in a moderate oven (350°) for 25-30 minutes. Put layers together with 1/3 recipe for Seven Minute Frosting, then ice the entire cake.

SEVEN MINUTE FROSTING

2 egg whites

1 1/2 cups sugar

1 1/2 tsp. light corn syrup or 1/4 tsp. cream of tartar

1/3 cup cold water

dash of salt

1 tsp. vanilla

Place all ingredients except vanilla in top of a double boiler. Beat one minute with electric mixer or rotary beater. Cook over boiling water, beating constantly until mixture forms peaks, about seven minutes. Remove from heat. Add vanilla, beat until of spreading consistency.

THE GREAT
FINNIGAN

And then there was Jack, the youngest of Grandmother Elizabeth's brothers and the greatest Great-uncle of them all, or so thought all of his nieces and nephews. When he'd hit the outskirts of Kamsack, he'd start honking the horn of his snazzy whatever-he-was-driving-that-year. Marcie and I would drop whatever we were doing, run out to the wooden sidewalk, or all the way down the dusty road to meet him.

Lean and lanky, his fedora at a jaunty angle, a wonderful, almost shy, boyish smile lighting up his face, he'd jump out of the car singing, "My ma gave me a nickel to buy ..."

"A pickle!" we'd scream.

"They didn't have a pickle so I bought some ..."

"Chewing gum!"

"*Chew, chew, chew, chew, chew, chewing gum, do I love chewing gum!*" we'd all sing together, as he'd reach into his pocket to pull out a handful of pale pink bubble gum.

With our mouths filled, we'd go through his other pockets in search of the round, shiny black jaw-breakers we always came up with. He'd give us one each, instructing that we make them last two days. The contest was on! Later, he'd take us to the Candy Kitchen on Main Street for boxes of Cracker

Great-Uncle Jack Finn, Pelly, Saskatchewan,
1920s

Jack, strawberry ice cream cones, chocolate marshmallow brooms, black licorice pipes and whips and red cinnamon hearts that burned our tongues. "The sky's the limit!" he'd say, winking at the girl behind the counter.

Jack was a confirmed bachelor. Great-grandfather Finn had set him and his brother Ike up in a small hotel in Plum Coulee, south of Winnipeg, near Winkler, Manitoba. When that business was sold, he set them up in a bowling alley and pool hall operation in Regina. Much later, Jack travelled through the little towns selling all kinds of insurance, as well as "sheet" (subscriptions to the *Free Press Prairie Farmer* and the like). Always dressed in a smart suit, white shirt and tie, Uncle Jack was a great salesman. He could and did sell twenty-year subscriptions to eighty-year-old farmers.

For many a long year Great-uncle Jack tootled along the dusty prairie roads avoiding potholes and the traps set out for him by all the Jewish mothers in southern Saskatchewan and Manitoba, not to mention North and South Dakota, who eyed him as a future son-in-law. It was not until he was in his forties that he was dragged to the altar, and then unaccountably by a public stenographer named Fanny, who was, as Auntie Ida put it, "no spring chicken and nothing to look at." What is more, she was a *kvetcher* (a chronic complainer), and it was not long before her nine sisters-in-law began referring to her snidely as "the *kvetch*." To boot . . . she was allergic to almost everything, even to babies. It was one of fate's cruel jokes, I suppose, that the Great Finnigan, who loved children so much, should be denied that joy.

Years later during my mother's last summer, as we were looking through the family album reminiscing, she told me another story about The Great Finnigan. In order to avoid being drafted in 1914, my mother recounted, he paid a doctor in Regina $250 for a letter stating he was lame. Then, she added with a fond chuckle, he went out and bought a fine Malacca cane and would limp whenever he remembered to.

MELTING MOMENTS

The rain is still beating on my kitchen window. Though I decided not to attempt Grandmother Elizabeth's Lady Baltimore cake, my reverie nevertheless continues, as I flip the page to discover yet another famous family recipe.

I am still that little girl of five or six in the dusty village of Pelly. The year is still 1938 or 1939. Next, however, I am standing in my Great-aunt Ida's shining kitchen watching her magic hands patting and rolling cookie dough into little snowballs, which she then places ever so precisely on a large black cookie sheet.

"Here is a fork," she says. "Now press each one flat. Like so. And now across the other way. Like so."

Feeling quite grown up with this new responsibility, I solemnly criss-cross each small ball. When I finish, she pops the tray into the oven of her old wood range. I ask, "Why are they called Melting Moments, Auntie Ida?"

"Because," she replies, "they are so rich with butter that when you pop one into your mouth, it's gone in a second, and you want more. Good things never last long enough, you know."

And as I was to discover, she was right, on all accounts.

When I visited Grandmother and Grandfather Shatsky in Pelly, as I did most summers as a child, I would spend a lot of time across the road at Great-aunt Ida's house. She was a termagant of a woman who had married my grandpa's milquetoast younger brother, Morris. When Grandpa, who was up by four o'clock most mornings, was having his afternoon nap and my frail Grandma was resting on the sofa, I would run out of the house, along the path bordered by a high carragana hedge and across the dirt road to Auntie Ida's, where I would be sure to find her in the midst of some activity fascinating to a little girl. She seemed always to be doing ten things at once: sewing, baking, ironing, wallpapering, painting, whatever.

Maybe this would be the day she would make an outfit for my Shirley Temple doll. Maybe she would be making cinnamon buns and would let me sprinkle on the raisins. Or if she were doing the laundry, maybe she'd let me turn the mangle in the little room off the kitchen that always smelled of sheets fresh off the line. Or best of all, perhaps she would be wallpapering the outhouse with pages cut from the mail-order catalogue.

Auntie Ida's two-seater was the most beautiful in all of Pelly, or even Saskatchewan. Its walls were covered with grand ladies in the latest Eaton's gowns, parading with gentlemen dressed in three-piece, double-breasted suits. Perfect little girls with clean and shining faces played with "Wettums" dolls or china tea sets from Japan. Equally flawless little boys pulled wooden wagons or rode bright red tricycles. Sitting there, "doing my business," was an adventure into the land of Eatonia, until the inevitable pound on the door: "What's the matter? You fall in or something?"

The grand master of cover-ups

Ida Shatsky, Pelly,
Saskatchewan, 1939

(she could have taught Presidents Nixon, Reagan and Clinton a thing or two), Auntie Ida did her best to disguise all things unmentionable or simply unsightly. In a corner of her kitchen, the Maytag washing machine stood totally enshrouded in unbleached cotton, on which she had appliquéd gaily-coloured flowers, and the pile of split logs and kindling, stored in an old crate next to the stove in every country kitchen in the land, was nowhere to be seen. Auntie Ida had Uncle Morris build a wood box with a hinged lid that rolled on casters which she kept on the back porch. And in her kitchen cupboards, row upon row of uniformly-labelled jars of fruit, pickles and jam, lined up like soldiers on parade, daring any Inspector General to find fault.

Like my mother or my grandmother, she might have been awarded the Good Housekeeping seal of approval. Her furniture shone, glasses sparkled, silverware gleamed and white dotted Swiss curtains ruffled around crystal-clear windowpanes. Her mahogany upright player piano, a Doherty, stood proudly against the living room wall, its ivory keys Pepsodent bright. Her handmade, white, crocheted antimacassars lay unrumpled on the arms and back cushions of the brocade chesterfield she had ordered from Winnipeg and a lace tablecloth crocheted by her own magic hands lay elegantly over her dining room table. Carpets and runners lay strategically over the scratchless varnished wood floor.

The only thing she could never hide was her disgust for Uncle Morris. The magic in her hands simply was not strong enough to transform him into something she could tolerate. How many times, I've wondered since, did she wish she could just throw a cover over him and stash him away in some corner. As a child, however, I was fascinated when I happened upon one of their fights.

"So you're thinking of putting your foot down, are you?" I might overhear her saying to Uncle Morris. "Well, we'll see about that." Shaking a finger at him, she would continue, "You just try putting your foot down and I'll stomp on it."

And as Uncle Morris fled past me out the screen door, letting it fly shut with a bang (something for which we little ones were always reprimanded), she would holler, "And if I want your opinion, I'll give it to you." Then, finally noticing me, "Want to make ice-cream?"

In no time she would have had taken out the salt, ice, cream and wooden ice cream mixer, settling me in the shade at the side of the house to turn the handle. There I would sit for hours, or so it seemed, churning and watching the bees work the sweet williams and the ants scurrying through the dry summer grass. The scent of warm hay, clover and manure drifted in from the fields to mix with the prairie dust and the warm, sugary smell of black-berries ripening in the Saskatchewan sun. And I would wonder what mysterious things Auntie Ida might be doing. Was she mixing some strange concoction from bottles and dabbing it on her hair, before crimping it to hide the scar on her left forehead? Was she pulling out the still warm guts from a freshly-slaughtered hen, carefully separating gizzard, liver and heart, setting aside any little eggs which she would later drop into the chicken soup when it bubbled on the stove?

One day I asked Aunt Ida to write out the recipe for Melting Moments. "Be sure to follow it exactly," she instructed. I took it back across the road to my grandparents' house and the next day begged my grandmother to let me make a batch because they were the best cookies I'd ever tasted. What I didn't know or understand then was that my grandmother and great-auntie were bitter rivals. Who kept the cleanest house? Who made the best cinnamon buns? Whose dill pickles were the crunchiest? I wonder, now, if my grand-mother was hurt that I thought Aunt Ida's cookies were the best, since she made all kinds of good things too, especially her white, downy-soft Lady Baltimore cake. Nevertheless, we made the Melting Moments and they were wonderful. So wonderful that I ran over to Auntie Ida's house yelling, "I made the cookies, I made the cookies!"

Letting the screen door slam behind me in my excitement, I repeated my chant, adding, "And they are so good, they're even better than yours."

"Better than mine, eh," she replied incredulously. "Did Elizabeth change the recipe?"

I shook my head, aware immediately that I had somehow blundered.

Auntie Ida paused, then quickly rescued me from my confusion. "Well, I'm glad you made them . . . and that they're better than mine." And she bent down to whisk me up and hugged me so close I felt myself melting, like a butter cookie, against her great warm breasts.

That moment, all these moments, long melted into time, are now beginning to resurface. To my amazement, an old family cookbook has become as much a book of remembrance as of recipes.

3/4 cup butter

1/2 teaspoon baking soda

3/4 cup brown sugar

1/2 teaspoon cream of tartar

1 egg

1 teaspoon vanilla

1-1/2 cups flour

dash of salt

Cream butter and sugar, add egg and mix well. Add vanilla, flour, soda, cream of tartar and salt. Shape into balls the size of a walnut and place about two inches apart on a greased cookie sheet. Press each ball flat with a fork and criss-cross. Bake at 350°F for 10-12 minutes.

GREAT-UNCLE MORRIS'S EVER-DIMINISHING THUMB

It is curious to consider that Great-aunt Ida was related to us only by virtue of her marriage to Great-uncle Morris. But she had such force of personality that no story of our family would be complete without her. Ida came from strong pioneering stock. Her parents were part of the original group of Jewish colonists who founded Wapella, one of the seven Jewish farming communities in south-eastern Saskatchewan in the 1880s. As is too often the case, little is now remembered about her mother, except that she was always either pregnant or miscarrying. Ida was the fifth of twelve children. Her father, Coleman Isman, however, was a legend (as was his daughter) within our extended family.

By all accounts, Auntie Ida's dad was a big man, over six feet tall, capable, but stubborn. Although he had a great sense of humour, nobody told Coleman Isman what to do, not even the monolithic Canadian Pacific Railway. When I was a little girl, I often heard the story about the time he and a friend hopped a ride on an empty flatcar to the small town of Whitewood, one stop west of Wapella on the CPR line, where he had business to transact.

It was their intention to catch the passenger train back to Wapella later in the day. That is, it was until he discovered the price.

When the CPR station agent took out a ticket and said, "That will be $1.25, Mr. Isman," Coleman went into a state of shock.

"A dollar and a quarter?" he asked in his thick Yiddish accent. "A dollar and a quarter to Wapella? Nine miles?"

"Afraid so," the station agent replied. "Besides, it's closer to fifteen."

Coleman Isman shook his head. "I'll give for you a dollar."

"Sorry, Mr. Isman, the fare is set by the CPR. I can't bargain."

"Vell, more than a dollar I'm not paying."

"Sorry, Mr. Isman. I'd like to help you, but I can't."

"So I'll valk."

And he and his friend strode down the tracks. A mile or so along they heard the warning whistle of the approaching train ordering them out of the way. His friend jumped aside, but Coleman had no intention of changing course until he had given the CPR a further piece of his mind. The train ground to a screeching stop mere inches from him, the near apoplectic engineer still pulling on the whistle. At which point, Coleman turned, shook his fist and loudly declaimed in Yiddish, "*Du kenst pfeiffen hynt bis morgen, mehr wie ein taler bazol ich nit.* You can toot from today until tomorrow, more than a dollar I'm not paying you."

It was this man, in 1904, who decided that his daughter Ida should be sent to Winnipeg to live with her brother and his wife, to help with chores and her nieces and nephews. Unfortunately, her brother was having a rough time financially and found it difficult to feed another mouth. His solution was to make his sister a match as quickly as possible, whether she wanted one or not.

The Shatsky Family, back row left to right: Sam and Morris; centre row left to right: Alice, Great-grandmother Shosha wearing a wig, and Great-grandfather Shmuel; Bessie, seated, Winnipeg, 1890s

Initially, potential suitors were not hard to find. Ida was a handsome young woman, despite a large scar on the right side of her forehead, which she hid beneath a deeply marcelled wave of lustrous dark hair. However, she was also her father's daughter and one may suppose that many a prospective husband had only to meet her to decide that domestic bliss might be more easily obtained elsewhere. The exception was Morris Shatsky, a nice-looking, mild-mannered, soft-voiced young man who, at the time, was working in the cigarette factory. She despised him from the start, but he was crazy about her and the *shiddach* (betrothal) was arranged.

Elizabeth and Ida Shatsky, sisters-in-law, 1906

In later years, Ida joked that when they married in 1904, Morris had thirty-five cents in his pocket and that for a honeymoon he took her out for an ice-cream soda. Certainly, she never came to admire anything about Great-uncle Morris, nor did she ever forgive him for inflicting four children upon her. To say their marriage was a stormy one is to indulge in extreme understatement. Indeed, for months on end they never talked to each other, except through a third person. Yet Great-uncle Morris loved her dearly until the day she died, in Regina, making hundreds of potato knishes for her granddaughters' double wedding.

No doubt Great-uncle Morris's standing with his wife was worsened, if that were possible, by invidious comparison with his brother and business partner, my Grandfather Sam. Morris was completely uneducated. He could not read or write anything except his name and was totally mystified by the intricacies of the English language, which played havoc with him all his life.

Being a "little pitcher with big ears," I overheard a number of Morris stories. One I particularly remember occurred during the early days of the Second World War. After listening to a noon hour CBC news broadcast on the radio in the Pelly general store which he and my grandfather owned and operated, he was reported to have looked up in amazement to ask, "They're going to win the war by dropping pantalets behind the lines?"

What a surreal vision: thousands of white, frilly, long-legged, ladies' panties drifting down from the sky like great snowflakes, landing on the turrets of tanks, on anti-aircraft guns and on the helmets of the German soldiers as they abandoned their weapons and scrambled to collect them.

"No, Morris," Grandpa Sam explained, "PAMPHLETS, paper with printing, telling them to surrender."

"Oh, aha. Well, that's a different horse, but it wouldn't help."

And he was right, for once.

Another story involved a New Year's Eve party at Grandpa Sam's house, where the entire family had gathered to ring out the old and ring in the new. At the time, the town of Pelly, the Province of Saskatchewan and, or so it seemed, the entire world was covered in snow. It was so far below freezing that the Uncles were soon taking bets on how much colder it would get, or whether an all-time record low would be set. I remember Grandpa Sam shovelling a path from the road so that everyone could dash to the back door and into the kitchen where the wood range glowed. Grandmother had prepared pies and cakes and other good things to eat and Grandfather had put out a few bottles of whisky for additional warmth. As I lay in Grandmother's bed, I could hear the strains of Guy Lombardo's Royal Canadian Orchestra, direct from the Rainbow Room high atop Rockefeller Center in downtown New York City, wafting through the house on gusts of dry warm air from the basement furnace.

Apparently, Great-uncle Morris spent the entire evening quietly listening to the radio descriptions of New York socialites, dressed in the latest fashions, dining and dancing, celebrating with champagne, crazy hats, horns and streamers. As midnight approached, the pitch of the announcer's voice rose higher and higher over the music and the noise of the merry-making until he screamed into my grandparents' living room, "Ladies and gentlemen, hilarity is reigning supreme!"

At which point Great-uncle Morris looked up and said to no one in particular, "Humph, what do you know. There it's raining and here it's snowing!"

For a man not known generally for quick thinking, however, he did on occasion come up with a sterling retort. Once, when he and Auntie Ida were in Regina visiting their daughter Bessie and her children, Uncle Morris decided to go see his friend, Sam Hirsch, who was serving time in the local jail for operating illegal stills on several farms around Kamsack. Uncle Morris took him the gift of a large can of tobacco and several packets of Vogue cigarette papers.

Hirsch was not exactly grateful. "What's the matter, Morris, they don't sell tailor-mades any more?"

Uncle Morris, a little taken aback, replied in his quiet, gentle voice, "What's a matter, Sam, you short of time?"

When I was little, the thing that absolutely intrigued me about my gentle Great-uncle Morris was the half-thumb on his right hand. I would watch in utter fascination as he deftly rolled a cigarette, spreading the tobacco evenly along the crisp white paper. Then, with a flick of that shiny pink stump, roll it up. In a flash, he had run the tip of his tongue along the paper's edge to moisten it, with the stump firmly along behind to seal it. A second or two later, he was inhaling blissfully.

How Great-uncle Morris lost his right thumb was a tale lovingly recounted on long, cold, prairie evenings.

Morris Shatsky, Winnipeg, 1939

Among their many enterprises, Sam and Morris Shatsky bought and sold large workhorses. Once, while looking over a possible purchase at a distant farm, Great-uncle Morris was standing with the halter in his hand, when the great beast suddenly bolted. Whatever the cause (possibly Grandpa Sam was poking it where it didn't want to be poked) and as improbable as it may sound, the rope somehow seized and half of Uncle Morris's thumb was literally ripped right off. There was no point in attempting to retrieve it. Micro-surgery was unheard of. All my father could do when the Shatsky brothers finally arrived at his office, after a four-hour horse-and-buggy ride back to Pelly, was to give Uncle a strong pain-killer, sew a fine seam on what was left of the thumb and bind it up with cotton gauze.

Pain, however, was not Morris Shatsky's principal problem — at least, not physical pain. Nor was the loss of half an inner digit. All the time my father was working on his stump, he kept moaning, "What am I going to tell Ida? What will she do when she hears about this?"

My father, using a little psychology, said, "Don't worry about it, Morris, I have a plan." And he proceeded to wrap more and more gauze around what was left of Morris's thumb. "Don't you say a thing to Ida. Just tell her you cut your thumb and that you have to come back next week so that I can change the dressing."

Every week for several weeks, Uncle Morris went dutifully to my father's office to have his dressing changed. Every week my father made the bandage a little smaller. His idea was that by the time the bandage was down to the actual size of the remaining thumb, Auntie Ida would have been prepared subliminally for its diminishment.

When at last the bandage was removed and Auntie Ida viewed his pink and shining stump for the first time, she regarded it thoughtfully. Nodding her head, as if she were scanning some long mental list of Uncle Morris's personal deficiencies — all he was not and would never be — and finding a little space at the bottom for yet another entry, she said, in her most practical, unemotional tone of voice, "Nu . . . so you won't be a stenographer," and stalked back into her kitchen.

THIS STORE IS NOT FOR BURNING

Of course, Great-aunt Ida, who never had a good word to say about anyone, especially hated her brother-in-law, my Grandfather Sam. For him she reserved the terms *momzer* and *ganef* (bastard and thief). As a little girl, I did not know what those choice Yiddish words meant. To me, he was a perfect grandfather.

When I visited, Grandpa Sam would take me with him as he made his rounds about the town. To the station to pick up a parcel, to the lumber yard for a board to fix the hen house, to the stockyard to check out a cow, or to the dusty and dangerous grain elevator where children were never allowed to go on their own. He took me along as he did his backyard chores: into the ice house where glistening frozen blocks stood on a floor covered with damp orange sawdust, into the dark and dank root house where potatoes, carrots, turnips, pumpkins and cabbages were stored, into the barn where he kept his chickens and multi-coloured tumbler pigeons. He showed me how, then let me collect the eggs. And when Grandma wanted to make chicken soup, he would let me watch while he selected a fat old hen, caught it up by its legs and carried it out, flapping and squawking, to the blood-stained block just outside the barn door where, in a flash, he'd chop off its head with a red-handled axe. The bird would flop to the ground, struggle up to its feet and run about flapping its wings in a last silent effort, looking about, as it were, for its head. Then, suddenly realizing it was in fact dead, it would collapse in a feathery heap.

One summer day, he dispatched a dozen or more chickens in this way. Grandma and Mary were "putting down" (preserving) chicken for the winter. It was Mary's job to pluck the chickens outside, her hands flying, her face lost in a cloud of feathers, which later she would wash and dry for pillows. Then Grandpa would gut the chickens, giving me an anatomy lesson as he went along. From time to time, he would let me put my hand inside to pull out the heart and separate it from the lungs and liver, instructing me always to be careful not to puncture the bag of bile, the contents of which, if spilled, would make the liver bitter and inedible. I also learned not to puncture the small soft translucent eggs which, when next I saw them, would be floating in Grandma Elizabeth's clear chicken broth. I also became adept at splitting gizzards and removing the sack of seeds the chicken had eaten earlier that day. Almost all the parts of the chicken, including the feet, would land up on Grandma's table in some delicious concoction which usually included a lot of onions and garlic. Later on, in the kitchen, rows of gleaming glass jars would be sterilized, packed with raw chicken pieces and filled with boiling broth. They would then be loaded into the oven where they remained until their contents were well and thoroughly cooked.

Grandpa also ran an egg candling station, where local farmers brought their eggs for grading. In one of the store's back rooms, dark and cool, the hired girl was transformed into a raven-haired high priestess performing a mysterious ritual, juggling four to six eggs at once over a magic bulb which revealed everything inside the eggs without breaking them. "See this small red dot on the yolk," she'd say, "it's the beginning of a chicken. Can't sell this one." And she'd put it aside with many others. Or, "look at this one," pointing to a tiny, perfectly recognizable translucent chick inside. "Can't sell this one either."

When in early 1939 my mother and father went to New York where my father had enrolled in a medical refresher course before they went on to Cuba for a holiday, my sister Marcie and I were taken to Pelly to stay with Grandma and Grandpa. When they returned, Grandfather started to prepare for the trip back to Kamsack, twenty miles away — not a trip to be taken lightly in mid-winter on the prairies.

He and Uncle Morris fitted a large wagon with runners and rigged a canvas cover over it. Next they filled the covered wagon with a sea of fresh hay, finally flinging clean wool blankets over it. "With a thermos or two of cocoa and a picnic basket," Grandpa said, "you'll be snug as bugs in a rug."

Samuel Shatsky, Pelly stockyard, 1938

The next day Grandpa rose even earlier than usual, while it was still very dark. "We've got to get going," he said. The winter days on the prairies were so short that it would be dusk by three in the afternoon, and we had to change our team of horses at a farm along the way.

Grandmother bundled me into a snowsuit and fuzzy cap, and woollen mittens with strings that ran up one arm, around my neck and down the other arm. At last Grandpa helped Marcie, Mary and Grandmother climb into the sleigh and we settled down cosily for the long ride. Grandfather looked like a great bear in his fur coat, his big hat pulled down so low as to almost obscure his face. In fact, the fur was probably bear, heavy and warm. At the very last moment a smaller version of Grandpa, my Uncle Morris, also dressed in heavy furs, heaved a metal box full of hot stones on the floorboards under the driver's bench to keep their feet warm. Then he climbed up and settled himself beside Grandfather, who handed him the lantern, took up the reins and growled a loud "giddyup."

The road was barely distinguishable from the surrounding snow-covered fields. When the sun came up, I peeked around the canvas to watch the trail of parallel lines behind us growing longer as the sleigh cut through the virgin snow, punctuated now and then by steaming piles of horse droppings. Ahead, the snow lay deep and fresh and uneven. Great slanting blue drifts had built up, often making detours from the road necessary. More than once the horses lost their footing. Several times we got stuck and Uncle Morris had to jump down into waist-high snow to push the sleigh, while Grandpa exhorted the horses to pull. By four o'clock that afternoon, we were again surrounded by a vast darkness. When finally we saw a few lights flickering in the distance, Grandpa joked, "I hope it's Kamsack."

Great-aunt Ida to the contrary, other people could and did say many good words about Grandpa. He was an articulate, soft-spoken man, fair and freckled, with curly reddish hair and a face that looked more Polish than Jewish. As a matter of fact, the Shatskys had come from Lublin, one of the oldest cities in Poland (although then part of the Russian Empire), in the 1880s. He was musical, loved to play the saxophone, and had organized the Pelly town band. He was also a great sportsman. In the summertime he umpired baseball games and always entered a horse or two in the local races. In winter, he ran the local curling club. And every Saturday night he listened for hours to "Hockey Night In Canada" on CBC radio, smoking cigarette after cigarette, while the almost hysterical, rasping voice of Foster Hewitt described the game, his excitement rising to an orgasmic pitch with, "He shoots, he scores!!" Grandpa, visualizing every move, hated being disturbed by anyone, especially children, while he was following the game. This was the only time I ever remember him being annoyed with me. The radio was in the kitchen, the hub of the household, so almost everyone who had business in the kitchen was told at one time or another during the game to keep quiet. "Can't you see I'm listening to the game?" This also applied to the news broadcasts. "Don't you know there's a war on?" The radio was my enemy. During Grandma's soap operas, she too would raise a finger and say, "Shh, The Road of Life," or "Shh, Ma Perkins."

Grandpa was considered so fair-minded by nearly all the people in Pelly that he was often called on to arbitrate or mediate in local disputes, along with Mr. MacKenzie, the bank manager and Mr. Dundas, the local black-sheep English aristocrat. The one dispute he couldn't arbitrate, however, was between him and Curly Ireland, which went on for years. Ireland owned the farm abutting Grandpa's on the Kamsack Road, and not all the fields were fenced. Early one spring morning, Jack Brennen, Grandpa's hired hand, discovered a cow missing and rode into town to tell Grandpa. The two of them started searching. In a distant field, they discovered muddy tracks leading to Curly Ireland's. The next morning, when he knew Curly would be out working in the back forty, Grandpa went to Ireland's farm to look around. He discovered his cow — its skin hanging down the inside of the well. Grandpa brought charges. Curly Ireland swore revenge after being found guilty and sent to jail. Perhaps as good as his word, but at least coincidental with Curly's release from incarceration, someone set fire to the new Shatsky Bros. general store in Pelly. Great-aunt Ida was the only person in the district who thought Ireland innocent. Grandpa was the prime suspect in her eyes, as he had been in another incident of arson involving another Shatsky Bros. store some years before.

After Aunt Ida and Uncle Morris were married in 1903, they opened a small delicatessen on the corner of Dufferin and Charles Streets in Winnipeg. Smoked meat and long sticks of *vurst* (salami) were brought in from Chicago and Auntie Ida, who was an exceptionally good housewife, a *beryeh*, made sandwiches, soup and waited on customers. She was definitely the boss. The deli, however, was not a great money-maker and when Grandpa moved to Pelly from Benito after the explosion in which Grandma Elizabeth had been so badly burned and permanently weakened, his parents persuaded him to take Morris in as a partner. Aunt Ida was not pleased, either to have her husband play second fiddle to his brother, or to have to live above the store while her sister-in-law had a comfortable house of her own (and live-in help).

Yet for all her grumbling, Great-aunt Ida, with her magic hands, transformed the second floor above the store. She painted the walls, hung lace curtains, displayed her wedding gifts and made the place a home, until tragedy struck. One night while she and Morris were in Winnipeg attending a wedding, the store went up in flames. Her *geschries* (screams) could be heard for miles; they reverberated through Regina, Yorkton, Melville, Canora and in all the little towns that dotted the prairies in between. She was convinced that Sam had arranged the fire, that he had hired an arsonist in order to collect the insurance money. Her attitude did not soften when Sam and Morris built her a new house across the road from Elizabeth's. Nor did she change her mind when a fellow from Pelly was caught, charged with setting fire to the store, convicted and sent to jail.

Grandpa Sam may have been no angel, but I doubt he was an arsonist. And he certainly was not a *momzer* or a *ganef*. The fact is that Auntie Ida was no lady when it came to the politics of family. But what did I, a child, know about such matters? As far as I was concerned, Grandpa Sam was perfect. So too was Auntie Ida.

Big Bessie And Me

The world may have been moving inexorably to war in 1939, but in the kosher-kitchens of southern Saskatchewan no one noticed because one was already raging between my two Great-aunts, Auntie Bessie (the youngest sister of Grandpa Sam and Uncle Morris) and Auntie Ida. In our family it became known as "The Strudel War."

Sisters-in-law Bessie and Ida had taken an instant dislike to each other from their first meeting and had became locked in a fierce competition over who made the best this, the best that, the best whatever; a war that ended only when Ida died thirty years later.

When Bessie made strudel, she would taunt, "Look, Ida, my dough is thinner."

"What are you talking about?" Ida would demand, her face flushed with anger, "I taught you how to make strudel. What I know about strudel you will never learn, even if you should live to a hundred and twenty!"

"Then how come mine is whiter?"

Voices rising, the sounds of their battle would spill through the house and out onto the street.

If Bessie made strudel with almonds, Ida would say she should have used walnuts. When she used walnuts, Ida would say she should have used almonds.

Sitting in my Grandmother Elizabeth's parlour one summer, Bessie, who was given to boasting, claimed that her Brown Cookies were better than anyone else's. As always, Ida was quick to challenge her. "So you'll come over to my house and make them." Bessie agreed. Another battle was about to begin.

Bessie sailed into Ida's kitchen and told her sister-in-law to clear out. She was superstitious and didn't want anyone watching over her shoulder.

When everyone was gone except for me, Auntie Bessie opened the cupboards and peered in near-sightedly. Organized beyond perfection, Auntie Ida never left anything in its original tin or box. She transferred all the basics such as Watkins Cream of Tartar, Blue Ribbon Baking Powder, Cow Brand Baking Soda, Canada Cornstarch, Sifto Table Salt, to clean glass jars, carefully labelling each one in her small, neat hand before storing them away.

Ingredient by ingredient, Bessie assembled what she required for a cookie that was to be adored by generations of children in Winnipeg's "New Jerusalem" and beyond:

AUNTIE BESSIE'S BROWN COOKIES

4 eggs	4 cups flour (approximately)
1 cup sugar	4 heaping teaspoons baking powder
1 cup vegetable oil	2 tablespoons cinnamon
1/3 cup water	1 pinch of salt

Beat eggs slightly by hand. Add sugar, oil and water. Stir well. Add flour, baking powder, cinnamon and salt. Mix until smooth and thick. Toss batter onto well-floured board. Cut off a portion the size of your index finger. Oil hands, roll into an "S" shape, dip into a mixture of crushed nuts and sugar. Place on a lightly oiled cookie sheet and bake at 350° for about 25 minutes until the tops crack slightly. (If too much trouble to shape the cookies, drop by spoon and sprinkle with sugar and/or nuts.) These cookies have an old-world quality in looks and flavour.

She mixed her batter with even greater care than usual. Then, like some modern-day Donatello, her fingers deftly shaped each precious cookie before dipping it into a perfectly measured mix of sugar and finely ground walnuts. Placing each one just so onto a cookie sheet, she paused for a moment to regard her creations with pride and confident expectation before popping them into the oven.

For the next fifteen minutes, she hovered over the stove, checking the temperature gauge on the oven door with the eye of a hawk. Finally, she peeked inside, "just to see how they're doing." Horror-struck, she let forth a cry of despair. Her cookies lay flat, hard and totally ruined! Tearing her hair and "*oy vaying*" all over the house to anyone who would listen, she was ready to commit suicide.

Ida, enjoying every minute, every splendid second of it, scoffed, "At least when I make cookies, they rise."

"How could such a thing happen?" Bessie wailed, rubbing one hand on her apron, while lighting yet another cigarette with the other hand.

"I'll bet you used icing sugar instead of baking powder," Ida smirked.

"What are you talking, all these years I don't know what's baking powder? And what kind of *meshuggeneh* (maniac) takes out from the can baking powder and puts into a jar?"

Auntie Bessie had a point, but Auntie Ida had won the battle. She would take no prisoners. Lifting a tall earthenware container down from the shelf, she offered Bessie one of her famous Melting Moments. "Now, taste that. That's a cookie!"

Although Auntie Bessie was a great baker, she was not beautiful. She was so far from being beautiful that she was positively ugly. Short, squat, with frizzy blond hair and a large wen on her left cheek, she was so ugly that, when I was in my Cinderella and Prince Charming stage, I could not understand how she had ever managed to find a husband. In fact, she married three times. It was only when I achieved a less romantic view of life that I began to understand. Her humiliation in Aunt Ida's kitchen to the contrary, she was an incredibly good baker. Her strudel and Danish pastries would have won first prize in any international competition. It was, however, her physical attributes that gave her the nickname "Big Bessie."

I saw her breasts bare only once. I was playing marbles on the living

Great-Grandmother Shosha Shatsky and Aunt Bessie, Winnipeg, 1920s

room carpet while she sat embroidering in a big wing chair. Most women hold their sewing or embroidery on their laps, but Auntie Bessie did not have a lap. Her enormous bonkers formed a shelf under her chin, to which she clutched the material. Suddenly, I heard her cry, "Damn it, they are a curse from God!"

I ran to her chair. "What is it, Auntie?"

"Look," she laughed holding up the needle, "I've sewed my tit to the doily."

"Doesn't it hurt?" I asked, horrified.

"No, not a bit," she answered, unbuttoning her blouse to expose breasts that could have hosted the winter Olympics. I gazed in wonder at this landscape of flesh from which she removed the fine thread that had been lightly caught.

For me, of course, she had other fascinations. The permanently crooked little finger on her right hand curled up in the most patrician manner over the handle of her tea cup. Transfixed, I would watch it as her fingers flew, rolling cigarette after cigarette, until she'd filled the red DuMaurier flat-fifty tin in which she kept them. Then, while her Danish pastry or some other mouthwatering wonder baked, she would sit, resting her breasts on the edge of the kitchen table, smoking cigarette after cigarette.

Big Bessie's first husband, Phil Bennet, was a handsome young man who, when she was a girl, lived next door to the Shatsky home in Winnipeg. He worked on the trains in some capacity, and wrote her long and loving letters. The family was not exactly thrilled about her choice since somewhere along the line Phil had picked up a drug habit and had served a term in prison. Bessie, however, believed him when he claimed he was cured and they were married. The newlyweds went to Pelly on their honeymoon. Unfortunately, not long after they arrived, my father noticed that the morphine was missing from his medical bag and Auntie Bessie noticed that Phil was missing from her bed. It was later discovered that Phil had other anti-social habits as well. A wife and twins were discovered in Calgary and it was suspected that a thorough search might reveal a series of other Bennet wives and children. The family tried to annul the marriage (this was cheaper), but finally had to resort to divorce.

In the meantime, Big Bessie's mother, my Great-grandmother Shosha, died in September 1933 (which accounts for my being given her name). Then

Bessie's father Shmuel, a poor shoemaker, died, leaving her the family house and what little money he had. If there is any truth in the notion that all heiresses are beautiful, overnight Bessie became positively irresistible.

Big Bill Labovitch was a large man whose flabby lower lip normally lapped around a fat cigar. He was manager of a needle-trade sweatshop on the second floor of a building on McDermott Avenue, the heart of the manufacturing and wholesale district in Winnipeg. He knew ladies' ready-to-wear, and he knew ladies. He had worked in the *shmatte* (clothing) business in Toronto until his marriage went sour.

Big Bessie and Big Bill were made for each other. She cooked and baked. He ate and ate. Every day he came home for lunch to steaming bowls of chicken soup with fresh *lokshen* (noodles) and chopped liver with fried onions and *gribenes* (cracklings), or velvet cheese *blintzes* (crepes) with thick sour cream, or spicy pan-fried *cutleten* (meatballs), or hot crispy fried potato *latkes* (pancakes), freshly baked cinnamon buns or Danish pastries and her famous Brown Cookies. All served with love, not to mention a little nooky for dessert. "Sha, I told you not to mention it." Bill had never had it so good. Neither had Bessie. He bought her a fur coat and the latest dresses and hats, all wholesale of course. He took her travelling. They went from coast to coast, by bus. She cooked and baked wherever they went and they ate until we thought surely they both would explode. They didn't know from cholesterol. They put their faith in Eno Fruit Salts. Alas, while at a Christmas party for his sweatshop drudges, Bill fell or, as Big Bessie believed, was pushed down the steep flight of stairs and died.

Her years of widowhood were spent visiting her sisters and brothers and nieces and nephews, or baking for a *bris* (circumcision ritual), bar mitzvah, wedding or *shiva* (period of mourning), until she met and captivated a widower, Mr. Aaron Gordon. On the minus side, Aaron was already seventy-five. On the plus side, he had a nice car. The two of them set up house in a small apartment in the North End of Winnipeg where Bessie flourished for a few more years until one day Mr. Gordon died, leaving her no one to cook and bake for. Eventually she had a stroke and spent the last few years of her life in an old folks' home, unable to speak.

What a woman Big Bessie had been! And what stories she spread about me. By the time I was ten I was known from Pelly to Moose Jaw, north to Saskatoon and east to Winnipeg, as a *vildeh hyah*. What a *vildeh hyah* was exactly I did not know at the time. But when I was introduced to relatives at a wedding or bar mitzvah, someone was sure to ask, "Is this the *vildeh hyah?*" A nod, and the relative would look at me and say, "Ah ha." "Is this the one that killed a cat?" someone else would ask. Another nod. "Is this the one who burnt down the house?" Again a nod. "Is this the one who stole the baby?" Again, a nod. Again, "Ah ha." And they all would look at me as if I were some creature in the zoo. This reputation as a *vildeh hyah* followed me until after I was married, but it originated from three separate incidents which occurred before I was old enough to go to school.

The first happened one afternoon when my friend Lloydene Moriarty and I were playing house under the back steps. Our dolls were sleeping soundly, tucked into their apple-box crib. Lloydene was busy setting the "table" with tiny china teacups and saucers for tea and cookies while I struggled Meow, our tabby cat, into swaddling clothes and a lacy white bonnet. Then, quite safe from her scratches, I held Meow tightly while Lloydene tried to force-feed her small pebbles that we pretended were beans. The cat began to squirm and wiggle, to scratch and tear and scream.

Lloydene was trying to pour milk down its caterwauling throat when suddenly we heard a voice: "*Vay is mir.* What are you doing to the cat. Killing it?" Big Auntie Bessie was peering down through the spaces between the steps.

"We're just feeding it," I answered.

"Well, it sounds like you're killing it. Let it go this instant."

"Aw, do I have to?"

"Yes, this minute."

Reluctantly, I opened my arms. Meow tore herself free from the long sleeveless baby nighty in which I had entrapped her and raced across the yard for the relative safety of the street beyond, dragging her bonnet behind her.

"*Gottenyu, gottenyu,*" Auntie Bessie muttered as she heaved herself up the stairs. "Such a *vildeh hyah* I've never seen."

No sooner had Auntie Bessie uttered the words "*vildeh hyah*" then they seemed to sprout wings and fly off in all directions, taking my reputation with them. And if any of our relatives, friends or acquaintances entertained any doubts about Big Bessie's veracity in this matter, they were dispelled a year or so later when the word spread that I had been caught stealing a baby.

That was the summer before my sixth birthday. Lloydene Moriarty and I were once again playing with our dolls in the cool shade under the back stairs of our house. This time, however, she had an "Eaton Beauty Doll" with auburn hair and blue eyes which her mother had ordered from the catalogue the previous Christmas and I had a "Wettums Baby Doll," the diaper of which soaked every time I fed it water from its very own baby bottle. We were so engrossed in taking care of our "children" that we both started with fright when Billy Clark's voice suddenly penetrated our world of make-believe.

"Jimmy see'd a dead baby back of the hospital!" he exclaimed, his eyes dancing with excitement as he peered at us through the stairs.

Lloydene stared at him in disbelief, then asked, "When?"

"This morning," Billy answered.

"Your brother Jimmy is a liar. Everybody knows he is a liar." Just the same I asked, "Where?"

"In the lane where they put the garbage. You wanna come and see?" he called, already halfway through the garden to the gate.

Lloydene was right behind him. "Come on, let's go," she yelled.

I followed, clattering along the wooden walkway, past our woodpile and two-seater outhouse and down the dusty lane past Fatty Riddel's house. I didn't look when we passed the Stockhammers' because their little son David had peed on me last week. ("Want to see it?" David asked. And before I could answer yes, I saw a small flash of pink and felt warm urine running down the front of my overalls.)

The King Edward Hospital was my father's hospital. I knew it well. At Christmas, my sister and I would help decorate the tree in the ward — a treat since we never had one at home. My father often took me on his rounds. I once watched him taking out a little boy's tonsils. The boy sat in a chair in the gleaming white operating room, his mouth open wide. His eyes caught mine, then wandered around the room looking at the bottles arranged on the shelves. In one bottle an appendix floated languidly; in another, a fetus. In another, a little bit of brain. I was familiar with all these strange things, so why, I wondered as I ran behind Billy and Lloydene, was I rushing to see a dead baby?

Billy was the first to reach the side of the hospital where one of the garbage cans had tipped over. He bent down and peered inside.

"Pee U!" he yelled, and leapt away holding his nose.

"What is it? What's inside?" Lloydene demanded, bursting with curiosity.

Marcie and Cherie Steiman, in front of their home, Kamsack, 1938

"Aw, nothing," Billy replied, greatly disappointed, "just an awful stink."

"Your brother is a liar. Your brother is a liar," I sang again and again, until he took off down the lane.

The next morning Lloydene and I took our dolls to play house in the sunshine on the front steps, where we pored over the pages of Eaton's catalogue.

"Winter will soon be coming on," I said, "and we will need to keep our babies warm. I think we should order these lovely woollen blankets."

Lloydene suddenly looked up at me and asked, "Wouldn't it be fun if suddenly these dolls became alive?"

"Yeah," I replied, then added with a wisdom appropriate to my age, "but you have to wish on the evening star."

As I changed the diaper on my Wettums doll, thinking about what Lloydene had said, it suddenly occurred to me that we could play with real babies. "I know what we can do," I said. "Come with me." We put down our dolls and carefully covered them. Lloydene followed me out into the street.

At the hospital, the waiting room was empty. Finney, the matron, was nowhere to be seen. Neither was anyone else. It was lunch time and the place smelled of boiled vegetables and disinfectant. We went into the nursery. I looked in each crib, finally choosing a dark-haired baby who was awake and gurgling happily. I very carefully stood on tiptoe and picked her up, being very sure to support her head. Cradling her in my arms just the way I had seen real mothers do, I walked slowly down the hall with Lloydene, past the reception room and into the lobby.

Lloydene held the front door open, but just as I started to go down the stairs, I felt a gentle hand on my shoulder and heard a calm voice say, "Cherie, let me have the baby, her mommy would be very sad if you took her away."

Finney was a large woman, who seemed even larger in her white uniform, a starched cap bouncing on a sea of hair like a sailboat in a storm. Her hands were trembling as she lifted the baby from my arms. "You haven't harmed her at all. You held her just the right way. I'll put her back in her crib. Run along home now."

"Wait 'til your pa hears about this," Lloydene said as she ran off, leaving me and her "Eaton Beauty Doll" to our respective fates.

When I got home my mother was standing in the doorway . . . waiting and very upset. Finney had phoned her. "You must never, never do that again. Do you promise? Never, never, never ever. Do you hear? I can't imagine what your father is going to say when he hears about this!"

I could hear Auntie Bessie clattering pots and pans in the kitchen and muttering, "That *vildeh hyah*. What will she do next?"

That was the longest afternoon I have ever spent. I wandered about the house, worried and scared, Lloydene's and Mother's words ringing in my ears: "Wait 'til your pa hears about this." "I cannot imagine what your father is going to say when he hears about this." Days passed. Weeks. Months. Finally I heard my father's car pull up and stop. I looked around my room for a place to hide. Under the bed. No. In the laundry hamper. Too small. My toy box. No room. Into the closet. I covered myself with a winter coat.

A few minutes later, I heard Father's footsteps on the stairs. He called my name, then entered my room. I pushed myself further into the corner, making myself very small.

He opened the closet door. "Why are you hiding? Come and give me a kiss."

"Everyone said I was going to get it."

"Don't believe everything you hear."

At these words, I flew out of my hiding place and into his arms.

He gave me a big bear hug and sat down on my bed. "Now, tell me why you took the baby."

"I was playing house with Lloydene. We needed a real baby. I didn't hurt it. I held it the way Mommy showed me."

"I know you did. And I know you wouldn't have hurt the baby intentionally but the baby isn't ours, you know. Even though I run the hospital, the baby doesn't belong to us. The baby has her own mother. You understand?"

I nodded.

"That's a good girl," he said, hugging me. "And some day, when you grow up, you'll play house with your very own baby."

I nodded again. But it seemed such a long time to wait.

One evening, not long after the baby-stealing incident, the sun was still shining brightly as I lay in my bed, trying to fall asleep. Like every normal child I hated having to go to bed early, especially in the summertime. Besides, it wasn't fair. My sister Marcie was still out playing with her friends. Just because she was twelve didn't mean she was grown up. After all, I was going to be six in just four months. I listened to the voices below. Mother and Father were sitting in the garden talking with Great-aunt Bessie, who was due to depart the following morning for Winnipeg. Snatches of their conversation, strange words in Yiddish, flew up to settle like birds on my window sill.

After tossing about restlessly, I flung my Wettums doll across the room and got out of bed. Crossing the hall, I crept into the big front bedroom, the one Great-auntie Bessie had been using. Her enormous dresses were draped over chairs like tents. On the dresser stood her large bottle of white powder with its white and blue label and the big red letters, Eno Fruit Salts. After every meal, I had watched her dump a teaspoon of the magic white powder into a glass of cold water and had never ceased to be amazed at its sudden fizzing and frothing. A million sparkling bubbles rose to greet her as she quickly threw back her head to drain the glass in one giant gulp. Then she would burp and say, "There, that's better."

Cherie Steiman, in Steiman backyard, Kamsack, 1938

Having looked through all of Auntie Bessie's finery before, I made my way to another small bedroom where a chest of drawers was littered with all kinds of things — tortoise shell combs, cheap jewellery, hair nets, stamps, old letters. And in an old cigar box, at the bottom under an assortment of curlers and pins, lay a single wooden Eddy matchstick. This I picked up curiously. To see what would happen, I ran the matchstick lightly along the screen that was on the window beside the dresser.

In a flash the white polka-dotted cotton curtains were engulfed by flames. I gazed in utter fascination for a second before becoming frightened. Then I dashed into my bedroom, jumped into bed and pulled all the covers over my head.

Mere seconds later, I heard someone lumbering up the stairs. And suddenly a voice screaming, "Fire! Fire!"

My sheet was torn off and I was pulled out of my bed by Great-auntie Bessie, who passed me down the stairs into Mother's arms as neighbours quickly rallied to form a human chain passing pails of water up to Father. Soon the fire, the most dreaded of all experiences in the heat of a prairie summer, was out. But all the while Big Bessie had stood in the upstairs hall waving her hands, shaking her head and wailing, "*Gottenyu, gottenyu. Vay is mir, vay is mir.*"

The next day, of course, she told everyone from Kamsack to Winnipeg what had happened. "It's a good thing I had to go upstairs for my fruit salts or that *vildeh hyah* would have burned the whole house down."

That night when Mother came to tuck me into bed, I finally asked the question that had been bothering me ever since Big Bessie had become a presence in my life: "What is a *vil-da-hy-ah*?"

"It means wild animal in Yiddish."

"Am I a wild animal, Mommy?"

"Of course not."

"Then why does Auntie Bessie call me that name?"

"Because she loves you, that's why."

How strange grown-ups are, I thought, as I looked up at the starry wallpaper on the ceiling and fell asleep.

Mendel's Children

I regret that I didn't know my grandparents on my father's side very well. Circumstances simply did not permit it. Undoubtedly the loss was mine, but one cannot love what one does not know. It is only after years of research, reconstructing their lives, that I have truly come to regard them as my own.

When my paternal Great-grandfather, Mendel Steiman, was born in 1846 in a *shtetl* as big as a yawn, near the Latvian village of Rezhitse, his father arranged a *shiddach* (a betrothal) with his best friend, whose wife had just given birth to a girl-child named Dova. By the time the two children had reached a marriageable age, they had fallen in love, but not with each other. Mendel loved a girl named Hannah Zelda Friedman and Dova loved a *yeshiva bokher* (a rabbinical student), who had come from fifty miles away to prepare her brothers for their bar mitzvahs. Nevertheless, in 1862 they honoured their parents' wishes and were married. Their son Solomon was born in 1863. A year or so later they were divorced.

In those days, divorce was no *shande* (shame). Dova agreed that Mendel should apply to the rabbi for a *get* (a divorce paper). This he did, justifying his request to the rabbi's satisfaction. He then went home, threw the *get* at Dova's feet and circled her seven times, repeating "I divorce you." Their marriage was over. Dova would later marry the young man she really loved. In the meantime she returned to her parents' home, taking baby Solomon with her.

Mendel Steiman, Winnipeg, 1920s   *Hannah Zelda Steiman*

Mendel married Hannah Zelda, a love match that would produce fifteen children, ten of whom survived. Their first son, Robert, was born in 1873.

By all accounts, Mendel was a good-hearted, gentle dairyman, not unlike Sholom Aleichem's Tevye. He and Hannah lived in Krasnoye, a *shtetl* just south-east of Dvinsk. Their small house, with its tumbled-down roof, lime-washed earth floors and thick-walled clay oven, was soon filled to bursting. In the summer, the little ones ran about the yard barefoot, happy as kings, unaware that life was *schwer* (hard). In the bitter winter they crowded around the clay oven and at night the little ones slept on its warm flat top. But even these few comforts had to be abandoned when the intensification of Tsarist restrictions against Jews owning farmland forced their move to the city. Consequently, Mendel and his family made their way to Dvinsk, their meagre possessions piled high atop a farm cart.

On the banks of the River Dvina, Dvinsk's ancient fortress had been built and was maintained as a primary defence against German attack. The city was also an important railway and commercial centre about 150 miles from Riga and midway between St. Petersburg and Warsaw. Open markets abounded in the centre of town, with fish and vegetable markets in the outskirts. The horse market was especially colourful, with army officers and Jews haggling with the gypsies and the *baryshnikes* (a mixed lot of horse traders and thieves). At the time the Steiman family moved there, Dvinsk's population was about ninety thousand, of whom forty-five thousand were Jews. Letts, Poles, Germans and Russians made up the rest.

The Steimans settled down in Pletzer, a suburb of houses with rotting beams and warped walls which, like a painting by Chagall, sprawled chaotically along the Riga railway tracks. This was home to about half of the Jews of the lower economic strata — workmen, casual labourers and small traders. Zack's match factory and Waldenberg's tannery were in this district, employing about 800 Jews between them. However, the lowest of the low — the underworld of cardsharps, thieves and prostitutes — also lived in Pletzer, in Na Peskach (meaning "on the sands"), near the barracks of the Ivangorodski Regiment. This was the Jewish red-light district.

As the eldest boy, Robert was making his contribution to the family coffers by the time he was twelve or thirteen-years-old. By necessity, he became a Jack-of-all-trades — now working in a brewery, now building or finishing a house. And in the winter, when construction ground to a standstill, he became a furniture maker. He was only seventeen in 1891 when the Russian mania for oppressing the Jews reached a new high. Once again, tens of thousands of Jews were forced to flee the country. And, as if things were not bad enough, Tsar Alexander III died in October 1894, renewing the collective memory of the pogroms that followed the death of Alexander II thirteen years earlier. The question on every Jew's mind was "What's next?" Robert did not wait to find out. With his parents' blessings, he set out for Riga to catch a ship for England.

In Liverpool, Robert found a job in a furniture factory, where he was to be employed for some seven years. The first record that we have of his progress in England, however, is in 1897 when one of his fellow craftsmen, Alfred Hornstein, invited him to his home for Sabbath dinner. The Hornsteins had had a difficult time since leaving Russia. Originally they had gone to the first Baron de Hirsch settlement in Argentina, where their high hopes of making a new life had been dashed when the colony failed. They subsequently emigrated to Liverpool in search of work. Whether the Hornsteins saw Robert initially as a potential suitor for their daughter Sarah, we do not know. Certainly, she was of marriageable age. At sixteen, Sarah was a beauty. Her soft, light-brown, curly hair framed a face with finely chiselled features, her dark eyes set beneath slim, straight brows. We do know that Robert was entranced by her. But if the Hornsteins were relatively poor, Robert must have been far from rich, working, as did Alfred, for the equivalent of a dollar and fifty cents a day (and probably sending money home to Mendel in Russia). On the plus side, however, he was unencumbered, young, strong and had a good trade. He was also very handsome. With his piercing blue eyes and sandy moustache, he looked like an early version of Douglas Fairbanks. So perhaps it is not surprising that as one visit led to the next over the ensuing months, he and Sarah should fall in love. God knows, they made a handsome pair.

Sarah and Robert Steiman, Liverpool, England, 1899

No doubt Alfred Hornstein sympathized with their determination to have a better life than England seemed to offer. As soon as they were married in March of 1899, he blessed their decision to strike out for California, where every Jew in Europe still believed the streets were paved with gold. Sarah was now eighteen and Robert twenty-six, although the handlebar moustache he sported made him look older. They bought the cheapest tickets they could find at ten pounds each, approximately one hundred dollars in total (or half a year's wages), and set out.

The newlyweds spent two harrowing weeks on the Atlantic. One can imagine them huddled together in the squalor of a steerage deck. They slept fully-clothed on separate wooden bunks, people above and below them. Robert joked about it and Sarah smiled queasily, until a March storm struck. Then, with heaving decks all around her, she thought she might die. Robert, sick himself, but fearing that Sarah's condition was indeed critical, tended her lovingly, feeding her sugared water drop by drop. When finally they reached Halifax, they were too exhausted to mind being herded through Immigration and onto a train to Montreal and Toronto. They had tickets for San Francisco, but instead of continuing on the Intercolonial Railway to Chicago, they were dispatched to Winnipeg via the same route my Great-grandfather Finn and his family had taken in 1882. The reason for this will forever remain a mystery.

On the Northern Pacific out of Duluth, they were befriended by a man who convinced them that he could get them re-routed to their intended destination. When they arrived in Winnipeg, Robert handed over their tickets and his new friend made for the ticket office. Robert and Sarah waited on the platform, but after a nervous half-hour became an hour, they realized their "friend" had cashed in their tickets and disappeared with the money. It would be forty-five years before they made that connection out of Chicago and reached the golden gates of San Francisco. In the meantime, it could have been worse.

The Winnipeg in which Robert and Sarah found themselves was fast becoming the gateway to the Canadian West as the transcontinental railway linked the vast prairies with the industrial east and reached out through a spider's web of branch lines into the surrounding isolated farmlands where Mennonites, Icelanders, Ukrainians, Swedes and Doukhobors were now settling. At the strategic centre of Canada, Winnipeg — "Gateway to the West" — was a hub of activity and was fast developing into the major distribution centre.

There were no furniture factories, but there were ditches to be dug, roads built, basements excavated, cement mixed and houses to be framed and finished. Robert, who was a journeyman carpenter and fluent in English, Yiddish and Russian, had no trouble finding steady work at a good wage. He and Sarah were soon able to rent a small house, and then buy a larger one to fill with ten children; it was not long before Robert was able to open a little hardware store on Main Street.

As the years passed, Robert's business thrived. In 1912, only fourteen years after arriving in Winnipeg, he became the proud owner of a three-storey hardware and furniture store at 541 Selkirk Avenue, called the R. Steiman Hardware and Furniture Company. Housewares on the first, furniture on the second, warehouse on the third. In March of 1921, *The Israelite Press* ran his advertisement: "Our prices are the lowest. We can furnish your entire home with the best furniture, carpets and oilcloths for the cheapest prices. If you cannot pay cash, we will trust you for the balance."

During the Great Depression of the 1930s, the second floor was

The Merchants Hotel-Steiman Block, built in 1912 on Selkirk and Andrews, is now a heritage building.

converted into offices for several Jewish doctors and dentists and the third floor into "Steiman's Hall" for meetings, banquets and weddings. In December of 1932, another of Robert's advertisements in *The Israelite Press* read, "Bring in the New Year at the New Year's Prosperity Dance at Steiman's Hall. Tickets 50 cents." Later, through an influential friend in the Manitoba government, he was able to obtain the last liquor licence issued before the war for the North End of Winnipeg, at which point he converted his entire building into the forty-room Merchants Hotel, with a beer parlour large enough to guarantee its success.

Included in the hotel's guest registers for the early years of its operation are the names of visiting rabbis from Chicago and New York and, in the late 'thirties, those of Austrian Jews who had managed to flee the Nazis. Of course, every guest also had to be properly fed. This was Sarah's department. During the war, the Merchants Hotel thrived to the point where Robert was able to sell it at a handsome profit. He and Sarah then retired to San Francisco, otherwise known as Paradise, where they lived to celebrate their fiftieth wedding anniversary in 1949. Robert and Sarah are long dead, but the Merchants Hotel-Steiman Block still stands, an officially-designated heritage building.

But I am way ahead of the story. Back in Dvinsk in 1904, Robert's brothers feared a repetition of the horrendous pogroms that had just taken place in Kishinev, a city of 50,000 Jews. To make things worse, the Russo-Japanese War was on the horizon and they were desperate to get out before they were called to serve the Tsar in the wastelands of Siberia (or anywhere else for that matter). Fortunately, the Canadian government was still looking for settlers for western Canada. Consequently, in 1905, Robert was able to bring his parents, Mendel and Hannah; his unmarried brothers, Max, George (also known as Israel), and Art; his five sisters, Sara, Rose, Mary, Annie and Tzipah; as well as Tzipah's husband Jacob Brickman, over to the land only the Icelanders called Paradise. (Sister Carrie would be born in Winnipeg.) Although my father was only seven at the time, seventy years later he was to remember well his father Solomon's house being filled to overflowing with relatives come to bid farewell to his Grandfather Mendel and his uncles and aunts who were setting off for "America." ("Canada" has never been an easy concept for Europeans.)

Robert and Sarah's house was always open. People were always coming and going. In the evenings, there were political discussions with Alderman Blumberg, who habitually left his hat behind and had to return to get it. There were singsongs around the piano. Robert insisted everyone join in all the old Yiddish favourites like "*Oifen Pripechik*" or "*Papirosen*." Neighbours would come for advice. They would talk in the living room behind the closed door. Mrs. Stokokoff came crying when her son Harvey gave a ring to a *shikse*.

"A *SHIKSE*! I'll have a word with him," Robert assured her. The next day Harvey got the ring back. Some evenings, all the Steiman brothers would gather to solve a problem. One of them always needed money, or was in some kind of a jam. As the discussion grew heated, their voices would rise, filling the house to the rafters. Sarah, ever soft-spoken, would clap her hands over her ears and say, "Oy . . . the noise, the noise!" But to the children, frightened by the angry voices, she would say, "Shush, sha sha, they're only discussing."

Of Robert Steiman's sisters, my great-aunts, I know very little. By all accounts the most interesting for me was sunny Tzipah, whose house was always full of assorted children, friends and neighbours. Whatever time of day or night, she would greet you at the door wearing a big white apron and a smile. Immediately you would be overcome by the irresistible and comforting smell of yeast rising. Kissing her, you'd smell cinnamon buns and sugared doughnuts on her cheeks and in her hair. Such perfume has yet to be bottled. Apparently, years earlier, Great-grandfather Mendel had hired a young man named Jacob Brickman to prepare Max for his bar mitzvah. Jacob promptly fell in love with Tzipah, a common enough occurrence among *yeshiva bokhers* in those days. In this case, Tzipah was not initially impressed with him. But on Mendel's insistence she married him first, and fell in love with him later.

Of my great-uncles, I know the most about Robert, Max and Art, and the least about George (Israel). When my grandfather, their step-brother Solomon, the oldest of the five, finally arrived in Winnipeg in 1924, the brothers arranged to be photographed. And here they are, together at last, nattily dressed in their best suits, white shirts with heavily-starched collars, sporting ties and lapel pins and watch fobs. Solomon's suit appears to be of coarser material, not quite as fashionably cut, but after all he had just gotten off the boat. Robert, front row centre as befits the elder statesman of the family, the successful businessman looking more than ever like Douglas Fairbanks, is gazing off past the photographer, head tilted, thinking perhaps, "Why, Lord, has it had to be such a long, tough haul? San Francisco could not have been part of Your eternal plan?" His brother George, to his right, is squinting off toward some distant place to which he might run. To this day, nobody knows what he did to make a living. He had no trade anyone knew of and seemed to move around a lot, following his fancy. He lived for some time in Chicago, writing letters to the family on Palmer House hotel stationery. For years nieces and nephews thought that he owned the place. He appears to have been the quintessential *luftmensh*, who lived on air and an onion.

Art, the youngest, was well-loved by my father. Short and barrel-chested, perky, peculiar and exasperating, he was an insurance agent. The eternal bachelor until he was past his sixtieth birthday, he was continually late for every important date, rushing from appointment to appointment like the rabbit in *Alice in Wonderland*. Arriving at our apartment for a Sunday turkey dinner just as my mother, Laura, was serving dessert, Art, with never a by-your-leave, sat down, tucked a napkin under his chin and waited to be served. Mother gave him a piece of pie and cup of coffee and that was all he got. Everyone laughed, including Art, who had a good sense of humour — a rarity in the Steiman family. Art told a lot of jokes, each of which he enjoyed immensely, always laughing harder than anyone else. Even when there was nothing to laugh about, Art would suddenly burst into laughter, making a peculiarly metallic sound when he did so — more like a bleat. It was as if he had just caught the punch line of some joke he had been told the day before. One wonders if he laughed a lot when, just seven years

The Steiman Brothers, united in Winnipeg. Back row left to right: Max "the entrepreneur," Art "the late comer." Front row, left to right: George Israel "the luftmensh," Robert "the elder statesman," and Solomon "the gentle exile," 1925

short of his old age pension, he was finally caught by a Rose in her late thirties, who could apparently run faster than a rabbit. Although marriage cured him of his bachelorhood and introduced him to the joys of fatherhood, Rose could never cure him of his habitual tardiness. Only once did he arrive on time and that was for his final appointment.

My Grandfather Solomon, the gentle exile, was sixty-one when he arrived in Winnipeg with his family, a little on the old side to start a new life. In addition, his health had been broken by prison and ten years of internal exile at the hands of the Bolsheviks. And although he could speak Yiddish, Russian and German, English seemed forever beyond him. A salesman in the old country where he was an agent for Böker cutlery, he would be a salesman in the new, making his rounds of Winnipeg's Jewish businesses and factories, taking orders for electric light bulbs. But from selling light bulbs he could not make a living. His son, Iser, my father, listed his mother, father and brother Boris, as dependants on his first income tax form in 1925 and continued to do so for many years to come.

Max, standing in the back row left, is the quintessential businessman, the busy bee, the "what-makes-Sammy-run" of the Steiman family: auctioneer, buyer and seller of anything and everything. Great-uncle Max had been apprenticed to a watchmaker in Latvia, but when the family emigrated to Winnipeg he found he could do better by travelling around the countryside to various work camps, isolated villages and farms selling, buying or bartering watches, jewellery, clothing, guns — whatever came his way.

Among Mendel and Hannah Zelda's neighbours was the Segal family. Aaron Segal was a baker by profession. Active politically, he was very influential in Winnipeg's Jewish community. One day, he called on young Max to repair a watch that had mysteriously stopped. It was because of this watch that Max met Rose, yet another Rose, the Segal's niece who was visiting from Omaha, Nebraska. Max was captivated. Curiously, he just couldn't seem to get Mr. Segal's watch fixed. He claimed to be mystified by its complex mechanism. Night after night, he would arrive at the Segal's house to examine its works, while making his own case to Rose. He was so in love that he might well have spent months staring absently at Aaron's timepiece had Rosie not agreed to marry him. When she did, Aaron Segal's watch began to keep perfect time.

With a little money borrowed from Rosie's family, Max set himself up

*Max Steiman, in front of the Busy Bee, on
Main Street, Winnipeg, 1917*

in a small store on Main Street aptly named The Busy Bee. And Max was indeed busy — busy running the shop, busy flitting over the countryside — buying, selling, trading, busy wheeling and dealing, always trying to make a buck. Returning always to the hive, to Rosie his queen bee. He opened a second store. Then another. Soon there were seven. Even one in Regina! By 1920, he was doing so well he could afford to indulge Rosie with gifts of fine jewellery, albeit he had picked them up for a song. His family, in the meantime, had also increased. In perfect symmetry, they too became seven: four sons and three daughters. Max, Rosie and the kids moved to a larger house at 135 Machray Avenue.

In another of the photographs, Max stands on the stoop outside his shop. One hand in his pocket, a black lamb astrakhan hat cocked on his head, he is leaning against a window filled with clocks, watches and guns. It is a cold day, but he doesn't seem to notice as he looks proprietarily over the bustling hub of the city. Up and down the street, his eyes search out prospective customers.

In October 7, 1921, he announced in a large advertisement in North End Winnipeg's Yiddish newspaper, *The Israelite Press*, his latest achievement:

THE MAX STEIMAN DEPARTMENT STORE

Men's, women's and children's head-to-toe outfitters
656-660 Main Street

Exceptional Bargains
The Greatest Price Cuts
The Finest Ladies' Ready-to-Wear

Max Steiman

I'm the man who broke high prices

Then, on October 14, 1921, *The Israelite Press* ran the following article:

> The opening of Max Steiman's Department Store at 656-660 Main Street gives us the opportunity to congratulate the young successful merchant. Max Steiman is only 33 years old and when one remembers that it was only ten years ago that he took over the small "Busy Bee Jewellery Store" which took up the space of only one small window on the same spot where now stands the large department store, one must be amazed at his development ability. This is the secret of his success: Max Steiman does not wait for business to fall into lap like rain from the sky ... he does not stop. He's constantly planning, working, advertising, drawing the customers and they come.

Unfortunately, only eight months later, in June of 1922, this same newspaper ran a notice paid for by the Registrar in the Court of the King's Bench announcing the bankruptcy of Max Steiman, merchant.

Max lost everything. He owed everyone. He had to put Rosie's jewellery up as collateral at the bank. Things were so tough for him that his daughter Esther remembers, "He came to the dress shop where I was working and asked me for fifty cents." His struggle to survive went on for many years. He and Rosie were constantly on the verge of losing their home. When the city turned off their water in the middle of winter, Rosie melted snow in big pots on her stove. But all through these tough times Max remained optimistic, positive that things would improve. And they did.

With the Depression came bankruptcies and mortgage foreclosures. The banks took over and gave orders to sell everything out from under insolvent businessmen and householders. Max scraped up twenty-five dollars for the necessary licence and turned his talents to auctioneering. He posted bills offering the buying public "the most daring, sensational auction sale ever staged," "the most spectacular event ever conceived, abounding in thrilling interest," "the most unique ever staged in West Selkirk." "If it won't bring in a dollar, it'll bring in a dime and I'll sell it for that." By combining the excitement of a Barnum and Bailey circus with Madison Avenue advertising techniques, Max began his comeback.

When an opportunity arose in 1935 to buy a furniture business from Joe Carter for about a hundred dollars, Max got it together. This marked the turning point in his career. From "Brother, can you spare a dime," he was soon able to redeem Rosie's jewellery from the bank. These he presented to her in a brown paper bag on Passover in 1939. Rosie was overwhelmed with emotion. She later recorded her feelings in pencil on that same paper bag, which she was to treasure as if it too was something very precious: "I got the jewellery back, first Seder night. I cried for joy. Sixteen years since I saw it. Some I forgot — I thought they was lost. Thanks to Max, my dear husband. He's giving me always hope. For sure, he is a hustler. We should only live a long time and enjoy the children." And they did.

Once more a successful businessman firmly entrenched in the life of the community, Max was not corrupted by this renewed success. When their neighbours moved to fancy new homes in more prosperous areas of the city, he and Rosie continued to live in the same house on the same street. Indeed, Max increasingly devoted his spare time and money to community organizations and philanthropic endeavours for which he eventually was to be much honoured.

As if one Max Steiman was not enough for Winnipeg, there was another lurking in the back of the family closet. When I returned to Winnipeg in the summer of 1989 to continue my research, one of my cousins casually suggested, "Ask Maxwell, he will know."

"Who's he? I've never ever heard of him."

"He's our black sheep," she replied. "Every family has one, you know, and he's ours."

Naturally, my curiosity was piqued. Off I went to meet him.

At eighty-nine, the other Maxwell Steiman was living comfortably with his wife Joyce in a new condominium. His eyesight was weak, but his voice was strong, penetrating, and his mind was as clear as a cold, sunny Winnipeg day. Like a computer, his memory contained every detail of every financial transaction in which he had ever been involved, as well as others he had nothing to do with. He turned out to be a veritable encyclopedia of the nefarious doings of certain members of our family. He had the goods on everyone. All I had to do was ask. He cautioned me, however: "Don't ask the questions if you can't take the answer, because I am not going to pull any punches." He was, in fact, the missing link I had been looking for.

This Maxwell had come a long way from the impoverished *shtetl* in Lithuania where he had been born in 1900, the third of the four children of Herschel Leib and Hannah Rhina Steiman. Drafted into the Tsar's army in 1904 just before the outbreak of the Russo-Japanese War, Maxwell's father, a tailor by trade, had to leave Hannah Rhina and the four children (Mary, Clara, Maxwell and Meyer) to fend for themselves. Somewhere en route by train to Siberia, Herschel Leib and his friend Mayerovitch deserted and made their way circuitously to East Africa, then to New York and finally to Winnipeg, where Herschel's cousin, Robert Steiman, was beginning to establish himself.

Meanwhile, back in Lithuania, Hannah Rhina managed in the way all those strong women of my family did — she carried on. She planted and harvested her garden, kept a cow, raised some chickens, sold milk, eggs and vegetables and looked after her children. Then tragedy struck. The cow fell down the well. Hannah Rhina flew about the village screaming for help, "*Die behayme, die behayme*" (the beast, the beast). Everyone in the *shtetl* came running, carrying ropes, blocks and tackle, heavy planks. They worked fast. Somehow the cow was hauled out alive, its bellowing drowned by the crying and *oy-vaying* of Hannah Rhina and all the other women of the village.

In Winnipeg, Herschel Leib Steiman, with a little help from Robert and a couple of Robert's friends, set up a small tailoring shop behind the grimy windows of 577 Selkirk Avenue, which he rather grandly called The Dominion Garment Company. In 1905 he was able to send for Hannah Rhina and the four children. By 1910 they'd added three others to their brood. Not long thereafter, his brother Haim also appeared on the scene and Herschel Leib took him into the business as a partner.

As the other Maxwell tells me, the partnership starts out on the wrong foot and stays that way. They need an inventory of cloth, so a three hundred dollar line of credit is arranged with R.J. Whitlaw Wholesale. Haim is sent to make the pick-up. He does not return. One, two months go by, no one hears a word from Haim. Then one day he shows up; broke, hungry and homeless. Against Hannah Rhina's vociferous protestations, Herschel Leib takes him back into the business. Hannah Rhina wails, "Your children haven't what to eat and you take in that good-for-nothing. Why? Why?" Herschel Leib looks up at the ceiling, then at her, and says with quiet exasperation, "I'll tell you why, Hannah Rhina. So you'll know why. Seven children I have, but only one brother. That's why." So Haim Steiman again takes his place at the counter of The Dominion Garment Company, meeting and greeting the customers and keeping the accounts, while Herschel Leib labours in the back, cutting and sewing until late into the night. For forty years the two brothers begin each day as they end it, screaming and cursing at each other in any one of several languages.

When Maxwell was five, not quite old enough to go to first grade (there was no kindergarten), his cousin Rose took him to Aberdeen School. With so many to look after, mothers were always pushing their children off to school before they reached legal school age. Everyone had to bring a dollar for school supplies, pens, pencils and scribblers. Every morning Miss Day, the teacher, asked Maxwell for his dollar. Every morning he'd ask his father for the dollar he never got.

Every morning he hung his head and said he'd forgotten it. Finally Miss Day stopped asking and he stopped asking his father.

To Maxwell, the most precious thing in life was his mother, so when he was awakened early one morning by his father and told to fetch Dr. Berkovitch for Mama, who was having severe labour pains, he ran like lightning the few blocks to the doctor's house and pounded on his door. Berkovitch was in his pyjamas.

"Papa says you should come right away, my mama is very sick."

"What is your name?"

"Maxwell Steiman."

"Where do you live?"

Maxwell told him.

"I'm not coming. Your father owes me two dollars," and Dr. Berkovitch slammed the door in Maxwell's face. He ran back home to tell his father. Hannah Rhina suffered all that day and night. Finally, the next day, Maxwell was sent to fetch a Dr. Kolikhman, who also lived nearby. He came right away, but it was too late. Hannah Rhina was rushed to the hospital by ambulance. The baby, her tenth, was delivered by caesarean section and lived, but Hannah Rhina died.

Maxwell never forgave his father for not calling the second doctor sooner and mourned his mother all his life. He absolutely hated Dr. Berkovitch for refusing to help his mother in the first place because of a lousy two dollar bill and he cursed the doctor publicly with every foul word he knew whenever he met him, until he finally drove Berkovitch out of town. Poor Hannah Rhina. She got a bad deal in life and didn't fare too well in death. The stone carver must have been drunk because he put her first name as Annie, misspelled Steiman and to add insult to injury added two years to her life. As to the new baby, Henry, he was adopted by Herschel Leib's brother Haim, who had married Robert Steiman's sister, Sara.

With nine children at home to look after, Herschel Leib quickly remarried and started yet another family (Chana, Laka, Morris and Rose). By this time, Maxwell was fourteen and just beginning Grade 9. As usual, there was no money for school supplies. He didn't like Fanny, the old maid his father had brought home to run the family, but he didn't really understand the new relationship until one morning, as he was getting ready for school, his sister Clara said to him, "If I ever hear you calling that woman 'Mother,' I'm going to kill you." That's when Maxwell decided to run away from home.

He borrowed a bicycle from a friend and got a job delivering parcels at three dollars a week for the Regal Shoe Store at 291 Portage Avenue. At first Maxwell thought his job would be boring and unpromising, leading nowhere, but in fact the very next day it led him straight into the hospital. Making a delivery, he was hit by one of the few automobiles on the streets of Winnipeg in 1914. Seventy-five years later, he remembered it as if it were yesterday: "I was in the hospital for three-and-a-half months and I had one visitor — one visitor in three-and-a-half months. With all my uncles and aunts and all my relatives! My father had remarried, he didn't need me. That was the way all the children were treated in those days. They all had large families. Not like today."

When he finally recovered in May, 1915, Maxwell got a job with another parcel delivery service. For pick-up and delivery within a quarter of a mile, the charge was ten cents; for half a mile, fifteen cents; a mile, twenty-five cents. At the time, the Bronfmans owned three hotels in the city — the

Woolsley on Higgins Avenue across from the CPR Station, the Nugget on Main Street and the Bell Hotel on the corner of Henry and Main. One day, Maxwell was given three shoe boxes to deliver, one for each of the hotels. The next day, he was told to deliver a shoe box to a prominent lawyer, A.J. Andrews of Andrews, Andrews, Burger and Fesido, the largest legal firm in the city. A.J. Andrews was the former mayor. It didn't take Maxwell long to discover the shoe boxes he was delivering did not contain shoes but bottles of Queen Anne Scotch. Prohibition had just been introduced in Manitoba and bootlegging was a flourishing business. Young Maxwell was kept busy, working twenty hours a day, sleeping in doorways, elevators, hotel lobbies. But he was also the natural fall guy for the operation. Nabbed by the police while making a delivery, Maxwell was charged with the unlawful sale of alcohol. Robert, the elder statesman of the extended Steiman family, bailed him out. At his subsequent trial, the judge agreed to sentence Maxwell to four months' probation on the condition that Robert guarantee the court that he had arranged a decent job for him. But what a job: cutting leather for jackets in his father's sweatshop, the Dominion Garment Company.

His Uncle Haim established a weekly quota, for which Maxwell would be paid two dollars and fifty cents, if he met it. But as he became more proficient and learned to cut faster, he soon surpassed his quota and rightly expected to be paid more. Haim, however, knowing that Maxwell belonged to the Dominion Garment Company for the duration of his probation, kept changing the numbers so that Maxwell, no matter how much he produced, could never earn more than two dollars and fifty cents a week. "So much for the love of an uncle," Maxwell told me. He might have added "a father" for fair measure. When his four months' probation was over, Maxwell's career as a cutter was history and, as they say, he never looked back.

By 1919, Prohibition was also in full swing in the United States, but as bootlegging and rum-running became more profitable, they became increasingly hazardous. In 1921, Maxwell again found himself an unwilling guest in the "crowbar hotel," this time in Portage la Prairie. Rumour had it that he was taking the rap for the big boys, the Bronfmans. This time, however, Robert was content to send word to brother Art, who was then managing the local Portage La Prairie movie house, to take Maxwell some cigarettes and fruit.

The result could not have pleased Robert very much. Maxwell recruited

Art to deliver five hundred dollars worth of booze — C.O.D. — to a connection in Chicago. Art, ever eager to make a buck, delivered the goods to the designated speakeasy but, new to the business, neglected to secure payment before the merchandise was unloaded. Afterwards, he apparently just stood about gaping at the local action, expecting to be handed the money due him. The minor mobster who ran the joint, recognizing an innocent at large, glowered down at Art, who on tiptoes was all of five foot one inch in height, and said he had two choices: "You can leave now wearing your shoes, or later, wearing a wood suit." Art chose wisely and was back across the Canadian border in jig time. When he eventually gave up running movie houses, it was for insurance, not bootlegging.

Meanwhile, Maxwell, with the enforced leisure to consider his options, realized he could go it alone, that he didn't need the big boys to be a successful bootlegger. If he was going to take the rap for anyone again, it was going to be for himself. He didn't mention this specifically when I talked to him but it seems safe to assume that he also decided he wasn't about to leave any more deliveries to the likes of Art, because when he got out of jail in 1923 (the year Manitoba voted to become "wet" again), he bought a large Buick and started doing the Chicago runs himself. His office in Winnipeg was a grubby, smoke-filled room with a chair, desk and telephone. His office staff consisted of anyone who could get down a name and address correctly.

One day in 1929, when his "regular" secretary found a better job, she sent as a replacement Joyce Koss, her sixteen-year-old German neighbour. A beautiful brunette, Joyce set in to clean up the office of Maxwell Steiman Enterprises Ltd. She threw out the trash: the empty bottles, the mountains of cigarette butts, the old newspapers, the abandoned food containers. She scrubbed the place down, waxed the floor, cleaned the windows, polished the furniture. The next day she brought flowers from home, put them in a bottle on her desk and hung a couple of calendars on the walls. On the third day, when Maxwell returned from Chicago, he couldn't believe his eyes. He hired her on the spot. It was his later recollection that he promptly fell in love with her. She, however, was not prepared to marry a bootlegger and such courtship as they had went on for nearly seven years.

Finally, on December 5, 1933, the 21st Amendment to the American Constitution repealing Prohibition was ratified. Bootlegging, as a lucrative occupation, was dead. In August 1935, Maxwell and Joyce were married by a

Justice of the Peace in Chicago. Soon afterwards, they moved into a house at the corner of McGregor and St. John's Streets in the North End of Winnipeg. And in January of 1936, the first of their four sons was born. (Gary would be followed by Curtis, Lionel and Rodney.) In accordance with their mother's religion, they would be brought up as Christians. Maxwell had long since given up all religion. He told me that more than anything else he had been influenced in this decision by the childhood memory of asking his father if he knew what the words meant when he *davened* (prayed). "You don't have to know what they mean, you just have to say them," Herschel Leib replied.

In 1936, Maxwell opened the Elgin Cafe, not far from Winnipeg City Hall at the corner of Princess and Elgin streets where, by his own account, he worked twelve hours a day — always willing to help anyone in need of a buck, never turning away a derelict in need of a meal but, he allowed, always according to his rules. As the years passed, he claimed to have done well enough, between the restaurant and certain opportunities, to dabble in private loans and second mortgages to send his younger brother, Mitchell, through law school. He also made certain that his sons received the education he had been denied. He kept in touch with their teachers and the principal. He got up early to walk or drive them to school. When they became discouraged

Maxwell and Joyce Steiman the day after their marriage, Chicago, August, 1935

about this or that task and whined, "But I can't," Maxwell would always say, and not very softly: "There's no such word as can't; that word isn't in my dictionary!" And in fact he did make very successful *menshen* (decent, responsible men) out of them. Gary became president of a large ladies' and children's outerwear business. Curtis went into construction and real estate development in a big way. Rodney became a tax expert and Lionel, a professor. "That's *naches* (satisfaction) for you!"

But to go back to 1935, the Steiman family did not approve of Maxwell marrying a *shikse*, and a

German Lutheran to boot. They considered him a black sheep. This was especially true of Maxwell's Uncle Haim, who was orthodox to the extreme. Haim Steiman was one of those deeply religious men who keep their relationship to God and man in watertight compartments, making it possible for them to love God while being totally immoral in so many other respects. Wherever he travelled, Haim took his own dishes and kosher food. One day when his son Henry (actually his stepson and Maxwell's baby brother) was walking along Selkirk Avenue, he happened upon a traffic jam, which was a fairly unusual occurrence in North End Winnipeg in the 1940s. Cars were backed up for two blocks. Horns were honking. People were leaning out car windows, yelling and shaking fists. When he saw that his father's car was the cause of all the trouble, Henry ran over, fearing that Haim had had a heart attack in the middle of the intersection. There sat his father *davening* in the front seat of his car, oblivious to the chaos around him.

Henry banged on the window and yelled, "Papa, in the middle of the road you're praying? You're holding up traffic and praying?" Haim pointed to his watch. "It's time for evening prayers."

Meanwhile, back at the Dominion Garment Company, cloth was in short supply. The Second World War had brought rationing. Haim was laying off cutters and screaming in Yiddish and Russian at Herschel Leib, who was returning the compliments in Polish and German, when the postman delivered a contract for Royal Canadian Navy greatcoats and a government requisition form for the necessary cloth, lining and buttons. Within weeks, certain gentlemen and ladies in North End Winnipeg could be seen sporting new, fashionable winter coats, all of them dark-blue. The shop was working to capacity the day government inspectors showed up to check the inventory. Not surprisingly, perhaps, they found a few discrepancies, which led to further discrepancies, which led eventually to . . . charges. Haim, who kept the books, was no Al Capone, but he was devious. He had himself immediately committed to the psychiatric ward of the Winnipeg General Hospital and stayed there until his lawyers straightened things out. "Everyone it seems has a price," his nephew Maxwell wryly observed, "even doctors."

Maxwell "The Black Sheep" Steiman was buried on Thursday, May 14, 1992 at the Green Acres Memorial Gardens, just east of Winnipeg. He and Joyce had chosen this double plot because "it's on the way to the lake so all the children and grandchildren can remember us as they go to their cottages every weekend throughout the summer." In this world of hypocrites, Maxwell forever had the courage to be inimitably himself. At the age of seventy-five he had taken a paper route in order to "keep in shape," becoming quite literally Canada's oldest newspaper boy, a story that made the national press.

There were a number of Maxwell's stories about this or that Steiman that I could have used, but at the risk of never having certain members of my family ever speak to me again. He was my missing link and I love him for his honesty and the strength of his character. Indeed, it seems somewhat ironic to me that his cousin, Max Steiman, "the Busy Bee," was so irritated at always being confused with Maxwell-the-bootlegger or Maxwell-the-gambler that in 1932, in desperation, he placed a large disclaimer in the *Winnipeg Free Press*:

> "Max Steiman, of 135 Machray Avenue, is not the Max Steiman who, last Wednesday, was fined $200 in city police court by Magistrate R.B. Graham, for keeping a gaming house."

It was this endearing and *meshuggeneh* (crazy) family that welcomed my father to Canada in 1912.

THE BOY WHO LOVED JAMES FENIMORE COOPER

My father, Iser Steiman, had a reverence for learning and a great sense of history. So when he retired in 1975, he enthusiastically greeted my suggestion that he record his life, especially since it meant we could spend every Wednesday doing this together. Wednesday, Mother went out to play bridge. We'd be alone in the house. When I'd arrive in the morning at ten, he'd have the kettle boiling to make tea, Russian style, clear with a dollop of mother's strawberry or blackberry *varenye* (jam). We'd sit at the kitchen table. I'd flip on the tape recorder and he'd start reminiscing. For lunch he'd bring out a tin of Baltic smoked sardines of which he was inordinately fond (Mother hated these), or herring with *shmetene* (sour cream) and sliced onions. Of course, nothing tasted as good as he remembered it did when he was a boy in Latvia.

He had been born in Dvinsk in 1898, a year before his Uncle Robert left for America. And it seemed to him that his entire childhood was punctuated by Robert's letters from Winnipeg, which was obviously a suburb of San Francisco. His father, Solomon, the child of Mendel and Dova Steiman, had been raised in a home where education was venerated. Dova's second husband, Solomon's stepfather, was a rabbi and in due course, Solomon would fall in love with and marry the daughter of a rabbi. The consequence was that although they lived in the same Jewish section of Dvinsk, Solomon's upbringing was light-years away from that of his half-brothers in Mendel's meagre home. Nevertheless, the two families were on friendly

The Solomon Steiman home in Dvinsk, Latvia

terms even though Mendel was conscious of the fact that, as an uneducated man, he commanded less respect than Dova's second husband in the Jewish community.

Unlike Robert, whose search for a better life would take him to Liverpool and Winnipeg, Solomon was to find prosperity at home as the sales representative for H.W. Böker, a German cutlery manufacturer in Solingen. Iser's mother, Etza, had been born in Narva, Estonia in 1875, the daughter of Rabbi Abraham Feigelson. She would bear Solomon ten children, six of whom survived: Lily (1895), Iser (1898), Mark (1900), Dora (1905), Bronya (1911) and Boris (1919). While it is true that they made their home in Pletzer, it is not true that Chagall would have included their house in one of his paintings. They were middle class. Everyone didn't have to sleep in the same room. They

Iser, Lily and Mark Steiman, Dvinsk, Latvia, 1904

dressed well. They ate from china plates, used stainless steel cutlery. Etza had a piano. The children had music lessons. When Iser and Mark reached the age of six, they went to *cheder*, a private Jewish elementary school where they learned the Hebrew Bible, how to read and write Hebrew and the fundamentals of Judaism. The girls had a tutor who came in the evenings.

The streets of Dvinsk guaranteed no safety to their large Jewish population and this was particularly so for young boys heading off at first light to *cheder*, or returning in the early night of winter. Jewish school children travelled in groups for fear of being attacked or kidnapped. In the past, young Jewish boys were often abducted by Russian gangs who carried them off to the Steppes, where they would be "adopted" by Russian Orthodox peasants who, with whatever brutality, would effect their Russification until they were fourteen years of age. Then they would be inducted into the Tsar Nicholas Regiment of the Imperial Russian Army, a regiment dedicated, among other things, to completing the conversion of Jews to Christianity. Those who survived to retire after twenty-five years of military service were allowed all the privileges of a Russian citizen, such as living wherever they chose outside the Pale of Settlement, except in Moscow or St. Petersburg. Although this practice was discontinued in the early 1860s by Alexander II, the fear it engendered lived on until the twentieth century.

Even with the collective memory that is my heritage as a Jew, for someone who has lived most of her life in places like Kamsack, Pelly, Winnipeg and Vancouver, it is difficult to fully appreciate the psychology of fear that pervaded the lives of my forebears in Russia. My father, for example, carried with him to his grave the memory of the morning at *cheder* in 1905 when the Rabbi told the boys that they would stop early that day. Iser and the other boys were delighted at the idea of a half-holiday until the Rabbi explained the reason for it. Seven-year-old Iser ran all the way home to find his mother waiting anxiously for him with her cousins, Nachta the tailor and Itzi the tinsmith, who were armed with knives. His father was away — "on the road" — as he was much of the time, selling his company's wares. "We'll stay in the house until it's safe," his mother said, as she bolted the door. The "Black Hundreds," a nationalistic group supported by the government which organized pogroms, were massing on the eastern side of the city. Another pogrom was about to begin. Possibly because all the young men of Dvinsk's Jewish districts had found something with which to defend themselves, on this occasion the enemy never showed up. However, the fear and tension of that time impressed itself indelibly upon Iser's memory even though, for the Jews of Dvinsk, fear was as natural to their day-to-day existence as eating bread.

When Iser was nine, his father had the good sense to send him, as he had Lily, to a Russian Gymnasium, or secondary school. Secular education at that time was hard to come by for Jewish children as there was a strict quota system. Fortunately, his father had the necessary wherewithal to buy him a place. A tailor was sent for and Iser was measured for his school uniform. How splendid he was to look with all those shining brass buttons and his jaunty *furazhka* (a peaked military-style cap). His hair was trimmed to regulation length — no longer than the average breadth of a middle digit (two cm).

The full Gymnasium curriculum involved an eight year program, with diplomas granted after the successful completion of the fourth, sixth and eighth years. When a student received the sixth-year diploma, he (these institutions were not co-educational) automatically became a non-commissioned officer in the army. School discipline was extremely strict, but the teachers, as Iser recalled, were excellent. The curriculum included Latin, Greek, German, French and Mathematics. German was taught by a German woman who refused in class to speak a word of any other language; French was taught in the same manner.

As one might expect of a rabbi's daughter, Etza took the religious education of her children very seriously. Every morning before Iser went to the Gymnasium, she sent him to the synagogue to pray. First he prayed, as the ritual required, thanking God for not being born a woman, then he prayed to God to give him good marks. At the end of the day, when he returned home from Gymnasium, there was a *yeshiva bokher* waiting for him to continue his religious training.

Given the temper of the times, a safe journey to and from the Gymnasium, which was some distance from his home, required a great deal of luck as well as skill. Animosity between the Jewish and gentile boys was so strong that Iser never set off for school without filling his pockets with stones, just in case. He had been quick to learn that the best defence is a good offence; if he even suspected that some other boy was entertaining the idea of attacking him, he struck first. He was to learn, however, that not even the best-laid plans always work out according to expectations. As he was walking with his older sister Lily one day, they were accosted by a young thug who threw a stone at her. Iser jumped on the culprit and beat him up. Lily did not appreciate his gallantry, for when they got home she told their mother that Iser had started the fight.

As a boy, Iser was no great scholar. His favourite authors were Charles Dickens, Sir Walter Scott and, above all, James Fenimore Cooper, all in Russian translations of course. *The Last of the Mohicans* especially fired his imagination. (After he died, I found in his library a beautiful English edition of this book bound in red leather.) He once told me that, for hours on end, he and his neighbourhood friends would recreate the adventures of Duncan Heywood and David Gamut in the backyards and dusty lanes of Pletzer where a Yiddish-speaking Hawkeye, Chingachgook, or Uncas would ambush the beautiful Cora and Alice Munro, played by Dora and Lily, tie them to a tree, then dance around in circles, chicken feathers in their hair, brandishing crude tomahawks, until Iser and Mark dashed out from behind a woodpile to rescue them. Oh yes, James Fenimore Cooper has a lot to answer for! Iser dreamed of the American frontier, imagined himself jumping on a horse and riding across a land without limit. The Pale of Settlement was not an acceptable alternative.

Iser also dreamed of becoming a doctor. It was a great event for a doctor to be called to a home in Pletzer and Iser had never even seen one until one of his uncles developed a severe stomach ailment that refused to respond to traditional remedies. Sickness, no matter how serious, was usually dealt with at home when Iser was a boy, hospitals being notoriously unsanitary. When any one of the Steiman children came down with German measles or chickenpox or any other contagious childhood disease, Etza would put them all together so that they would all catch it and get it over with. But even in a family such as theirs with relatively decent sanitation and good nutrition, four of Iser's younger brothers and sisters died of one sickness or another.

Iser related his own fascination with medicine to the occasion when, at the age of five or six, he developed an abscess under his arm and Etza decided to take him to be looked at by a *feldscher*, a Russian field-surgeon. The lancing of this abscess was one of those seemingly trivial events that turn out to have a lasting effect on one's life. The doctor was a kindly man, told him about his profession and how he had trained in Germany. How, if he wanted, Iser could become a doctor when he grew up.

While Etza was paying him, Iser stood beside the fence which bordered the *feldscher's* garden, feeling pretty miserable until he noticed a kopeck that someone had dropped in the road. In a second he forgot his pain and pocketed the money. On the way back home Etza allowed him to spend it on his favourite candy, jellied chocolates. Years later he would make sure he had a good supply of barley sugar candies for his little patients.

In the fall of 1912, the year that he became fourteen, Iser received his

fourth-year Gymnasium diploma. Although this entitled him to certain privileges at school that he had not enjoyed before, he had no desire to continue
living in Dvinsk. When it came time to register for his fifth year, he simply
refused. He wanted to finish his studies in America, specifically in Winnipeg
where Uncle Robert and Grandfather Mendel lived. Failing that, he would
get a job, any job; he was not going back to the Gymnasium! Whether he had
simply had enough of the anti-Semitic diatribes of his teachers or the racist
slurs of his fellow students, I do not know. By the time I had thought of these
questions, my father was no longer alive to answer them. Certainly, I am prepared to grant that James Fenimore Cooper cannot be held entirely responsible for his decision. Nor can I explain the absence of traditional parental
authority in Solomon Steiman's home. The fact that Iser was technically a
man — it was almost a year since his bar mitzvah — should not have made
any difference. Normally, a Jewish father's word was law. Period. Do what
you're told. No questions allowed. Whatever the circumstances, when Solomon realized how determined Iser was, he relented, so far as his son not returning to the Gymnasium was concerned. He then tried to convince Iser to
study in Germany or France or even England instead, saying, "Who goes
there but bankrupts, embezzlers and good-for-nothings who could not 'make
it' in Russia?" To many left behind in Russia, a person gone to America was as
good as dead. And Iser was his first-born son. At last he gave in entirely and
wrote Robert to make arrangements. Robert agreed to provide Iser board
and room and the opportunity to attend high school. Solomon agreed to send
Robert fifty dollars a month, reckoning that it was not much more than he
would have paid in Gymnasium tuition. Then he went to see the Secretary of
the District in order to obtain Iser's release from military service. In those days
it was possible to be exempted from military service by paying "recruiting
money," sometimes as much as one thousand rubles per recruit. More money
changed hands. Next came the passport, which also did not come cheap. At
home, Etza arranged for a tailor to measure Iser for a suit and a coat and for a
shoemaker to make him boots. Since they didn't know what kind of hats were
worn in Canada, she decided his Gymnasium cap would do.

Lily watched these preparations with an excitement mixed with envy.
"Why can't I go too, Papa?"

Etza was overcome by sadness and beset by countless fears. "What if...?
What if . . . ?"

To which Iser would reply, "Don't worry Mama, don't worry."

Before leaving Russia, Iser went by train to visit his grandfather, Rabbi Abraham Feigelson, in Narva, not far from St. Petersburg. When Iser told him he was leaving for Canada, his grandfather gave him some unusually enlightened advice for a rabbi of that time. "My boy, you will be living amongst strangers and you must remember that when a stranger offers you the privilege of eating at his table, you must respect his customs and eat his food. If you are invited to eat with a gentile, it is not considered a sin to remove your hat. You may take your hat off out of respect for your host. You may find yourself at a table with food that is forbidden to us. You can avoid those foods if you know about them but if you don't, do not insult your host by refusing them. It is more important to respect other people's customs and their ways of life than to persist in your own ways and customs. People abuse the privileges of their religious training or customs and show disrespect for others by inflicting them on unwilling neighbours, as well as throwing doubt on one's own intelligence." Iser would have reason to recall these words many times over in the years to come.

By the middle of November, all the preparations for his departure were complete. At the train station in Dvinsk, he said goodbye to his mother and sisters, who sobbed bitterly, while brother Mark acted the brave young man. His mother handed him a large package of kosher food as she was worried that there would be none available on the long trip. Solomon accompanied Iser by train to the Baltic seaport of Libau, about two hundred miles from Dvinsk. There, before he boarded a ship for Hull, England, whence he would sail to Canada, they went to a photographer for what they both must have supposed was a final remembrance of their lives together.

Against a backdrop of leafy trees, Solomon sits on a rustic bench in his black, double-breasted coat with the

Great-grandfather Rabbi Abraham Feigelson, Narva, Estonia, circa 1860

velvet collar. He's wearing a broad-brimmed black velour fedora and fine black leather gloves. Iser, handsome even at fourteen, stands at his side in his new, long, single-breasted coat and his impressive Gymnasium cap with its wide band of ribbon, gold crest and shiny black patent leather peak. His hand rests on Solomon's arm reassuringly, but his lips are slightly tremulous. Solomon, meticulously barbered, his moustache twirled and waxed, his goatee trimmed to a neat rectangle, looks out through his thick glasses, heavy-lidded, serious, reluctantly resigned to his son's imminent departure.

Iser and Solomon Steiman, Libau, Latvia, November 1912

After embracing Iser at the dock, Solomon imparted his final bit of fatherly wisdom: "Guard that passport, it's like gold." And Iser kept it in a safe place all his life.

The first leg of Iser's journey was miserable, even though everyone in steerage was most kind and helpful to him. To them he was someone special, a student from the Gymnasium. And all alone. At Hull, once he got his land legs back, he was able to go sightseeing, looking into the shop windows — marvelling at the tall buildings. He later would remember being amazed at the displays of fresh vegetables and fruit in the stores and he recalled buying an apple to share with a friend from the ship. That night at the Jewish immigration hall, they were served a good kosher meal of potatoes and herring, which he heartily ate. The following morning they boarded the train for Liverpool, where they boarded ship for Canada.

Feeling queasy during the first night out, he was about to rise from his lower bunk when a gush of vomit landed on his head. With a few choice Russian and Yiddish curses he had not learned in the Gymnasium or *cheder*, he wiped himself off and dragged his body up to the deck where, clinging to the rail, he heaved his guts into the relentless and unforgiving sea. The frightful crossing took eight days and he never forgot it. The second time he dragged himself up on deck was when the ship entered the calm waters of Halifax harbour.

Everyone stayed in the immigration hall overnight, cleared customs in the morning and boarded the train for the Wild West. It was colonist class all the way with only wooden benches to stretch out on, but he made himself as comfortable as he could. The greatest wonder and surprise to him were the lighted store windows in the towns along the railway line. In Dvinsk, every store was closed at night, shuttered up and bolted down. He thought the people of Canada extremely foolish to tempt thieves in this way. When at last the train pulled into Winnipeg station, Uncle Robert and Aunt Sarah were waiting for him. They recognized him by his Gymnasium cap, now a little worse for the journey.

Uncle Robert by this time had established a second small hardware store on Selkirk Avenue in the North End of the city and it soon became apparent to Iser that he was expected to help out there after school and on the weekends, despite the fact that Solomon was sending money for his room and board. When the world went to war in 1914, however, Solomon was exiled to Siberia and all contact with him ceased. Iser had now to find the money to pay for his room and board or move out. Fortunately, after little more than a year in Winnipeg, he had begun giving English lessons to the newer immigrants. He had a Russian accent you could cut with a saw, but he went confidently off to his students' homes in the evenings, often earning himself as much as sixteen or eighteen dollars a month.

When he could not pay his board to Uncle Robert and Aunt Sarah, he would go to stay with Grandfather Mendel Steiman. Many an evening when he returned from tutoring, he would find his grandfather nodding over some advanced Hebrew commentary that Mendel would never be able to understand. It was one of the greatest disappointments of Mendel's life not to be able to keep up with his contemporaries at the synagogue. Still, he would go there and sit with the scholars, listening, reaching out for knowledge, which like all Jews he valued so highly. It was a moment of high achievement for him when he was invited to sit on the synagogue's *kashruth* committee, which was concerned with the strict observance of the Jewish dietary code.

In St. John's High School, Iser proved to be just an average student except in languages, where he excelled. But he loved it anyway and was very disappointed when he had to leave to go to work full-time one year short of graduation. But war had broken out and it was impossible for Solomon to transfer funds. Uncle Robert had opened a branch store on Logan Avenue West and asked Iser to "manage" it. Robert's sister Mary, however, was to look after the stock and the books. In 1915, winter came even earlier than usual to Winnipeg. By the middle of October, Iser was shovelling away the snow in front of the store, building up the fire in the pot-bellied stove and more often than not, doing little else. Some days there were no customers at all. Just before Christmas on a very dull, cold day, he fell asleep in front of the stove and dreamed a terrible dream. He awoke in a fright. He had seen himself as an old man, still selling nails and stovepipes. He got up, put on his coat and set off uptown to Main Street, then kept right on until he got to St. John's High School where he met with the principal, Mr. Campbell, and one of his former teachers, Mr. Cornish.

Iser told them he wanted to study on his own and write the university entrance exams in June. He wanted to go to medical school. Cornish said regulations stipulated school attendance but that they would make an exception. They would provide him all the texts and curriculum materials, although Iser would have to attend school for the month of May before writing the exams.

"It will be a lot of work," Cornish warned him. "How will you do all this and manage the store?"

Iser replied that because business was very slow, he could find time during the day and that he had a couple of friends who would help him study in the evenings.

"If you want to make the quota you'll need to get top marks," Cornish warned.

It was well-known, within the Jewish community as well as outside it, that there were implicit quotas on the number of Jewish students accepted by the country's medical schools. There were also quotas restricting women and other ethnic minorities. Moreover, Jews were not appointed to important positions in Manitoba. There were no Jewish judges, no Jewish professors. Jews were banned from joining some private clubs and from living in certain residential areas of Winnipeg. And such Jewish doctors as the university graduated could not get hospital appointments. This iniquitous system would not be rescinded until 1945.

In May, Iser returned to high school and in June he was allowed to write his examinations, as promised. His marks were first class in every subject. He was accepted by the University of Manitoba that September of 1916. He'd made the quota. Always a romantic, Iser was caught up immediately at university by the war-time idealism and patriotic fervour that pervaded the campus. The world had to be made safe for democracy. Germany had to be defeated. Britain, France and Russia had to triumph. Canada needed him to help make this happen. Iser and his friends answered the call of "King and Country." They joined the Canadian Officers Training Corps.

Possibly Iser didn't know that the First World War had settled long since into the horrors of trench warfare, or that the flower of Canada's young manhood was being senselessly sacrificed. Still, however skewed the press reports by government propaganda, it was common knowledge that casualties were high. The Battle of the Somme raged from the beginning of July until mid-November 1916, at a cost of over 400,000 British (including 24,000 Canadian), 200,000 French and 400,000 to 500,000 German dead and wounded. Figures like these cannot be kept secret long. But hard as it may be for a generation now so far removed in time to imagine, these students at the University of Manitoba were still filled with flag-waving zeal. Joining the Canadian Officers Training Corps (COTC) meant being issued a smart uniform, martial music, marching on the university parade ground to the admiration of the other students (particularly those of the female persuasion) and looking forward to the glories of war. James Fenimore Cooper would have approved. Iser, however, was obliged to keep his COTC uniform at the university. Grandfather Mendel did not approve; he had fundamental philosophic and moral objections to military service.

As Iser recalled it many years later, "At Christmas 1916, the officer in charge of our company lined us up, called us to attention and said: 'Gentlemen, the 196th University Battalion is going overseas. Those wishing to volunteer . . . ONE STEP FORWARD!'" Iser and his friends stepped forward to a man. Told to report immediately to the COTC office, they were provided the appropriate forms. The following day, however, when Iser returned with his completed papers, the Adjutant informed him that because he was only eighteen-years-old and not a British subject, he required the permission of his parents or guardian before he could be placed on the active service roster. Iser explained that his parents were somewhere in Russia, that he hadn't heard from them for more than two years and that, given their strong views on the subject, there was no way he could ask his Uncle Robert or Grandfather to sign for him. The Adjutant could only express his regrets. Regulations were regulations. So Iser had to watch as his friends marched off to the glories they all imagined awaited them in France.

News from the front filled the newspapers every day. Iser was distressed. As he was writing his exams in the spring of 1917, his friends were part of the heroic Canadian force that took Vimy Ridge. While he was working for Uncle Robert that summer, his friends were fighting and dying at Passchendaele. He decided that he could not in conscience go back to university in the fall, but must find a job that would allow him the opportunity to serve his new country in a meaningful way. One of the officials in the Manitoba Department of Education, Mr. Ira Strachan, convinced Iser that he had a teaching post available in one of the more isolated corners of the province that would test the mettle of any patriot.

The one-room Moose Bay School (Grades 1 to 8) was forty miles by rough road from the nearest railway station at The Pas, the closest town. The nearest store was seven miles away. The price of food was sky high because of the inaccessibility of the place. And the mail, when it happened to get through, was delivered by horse and buggy or sleigh. The school district's population was nearly one hundred per cent Ukrainian — farmers whose strongly anti-Russian heritage had resulted in the public expression of pro-German sympathies during the war. In fact, they had torn down the Union Jack from over the school and had refused to send their children to be taught by the previous teacher, Mr. Croydon, an Englishman. Iser accepted the challenge.

When he arrived at the Moose Bay School in late August 1917, however, Mr. Croydon was still living in the log cabin provided by the school district as accommodation for the teacher. He and his wife, a tall Irishwoman, had yet to complete the house they were building for themselves on their homestead a distance away. Although the log cabin had but one large room, Iser felt he could not say to them, "Get out, this is my place now." The Croydons had little money and there was no other place for them to go. Besides, he thought, living with them might have certain advantages: their food might not be kosher, but he didn't know how to cook at all; he could improve his English pronunciation by listening to them; and he could experience a different cultural ambience — Iser, at nineteen years of age, had never lived so much as a day in a gentile household. So he agreed to pay Mrs. Croydon board; and at night, they partitioned the room with a line and a couple of blankets for the purposes of privacy.

After a week, Iser realized that Mrs. Croydon couldn't cook any better than he could. In addition, she seemed determined to feed the three of them on what little he paid her. He was starving. At the same time he realized that he had no choice. The nearest English-speaking family was miles away and although he could have lived with one of the Ukrainian families, he knew this was potentially poor policy. As the teacher (by definition a person of considerable authority and influence in any community in 1918), he had to remain neutral and friendly towards all.

Iser took to spending more and more time at the school, which was only fifty feet away from the log cabin, where he would stoke up the little potbelly stove and settle down for the evening. Although he had never been so hungry, he was at least warm. The Croydons were so parsimonious that they objected to keeping their fire burning after the evening meal, even though the wood was provided gratis by the school district. One Saturday in January, Croydon took Iser to see his house. It was huge, with an attic in the English style, but he had done little more than frame it up. Only one part of it was completely enclosed and Iser could see that it was going to take a long time for him to finish it.

But with spring came hope. While out walking one Saturday some three or four miles from the school, he was hailed by an elderly farmer named Sanders, one of the few English-speaking people in the district, who was out mending a fence. Iser stopped to chat and was invited in for lunch. Sanders shared his home with his housekeeper, Mrs. Agnes Greatam, and her little boy. The meal Mrs. Greatam served that day was the best Iser had eaten in months. And then, when he was about to leave, she pressed a loaf of bread into his hands. "I hope you aren't offended by me offering you a loaf of bread," she said, "but I know Mrs. Croydon hasn't the facilities."

The next Saturday, Iser went to visit Mr. Sanders again, coincidentally at lunch time. His welcome was such that he asked Sanders if it would be possible for him to come and spend his weekends with them. "I will gladly pay board," he volunteered, "but you must understand that I am starving!"

"Oh, for goodness sake, lad, you are more than welcome. Why don't you move?"

Iser rushed back to the Croydons, told them he had to move because of his health (which was true), and was ensconced in the Sanders' house by suppertime.

Before taking up his position at Moose Bay School, Iser had attended a course at the normal school in Winnipeg given by Dr. Sisler, who had written a book on how to teach foreign-language students. His theories were hardly revolutionary. In fact, they simply confirmed the wisdom of Iser's German and French teachers at the Gymnasium in Dvinsk. The consequence was that before he ever saw his students, he had made up his mind not to speak a word of Ukrainian to them during school hours. Prior to Mr. Croydon, the Ukrainian school trustees had always hired teachers of Ukrainian origin for the school. Iser decided that his goals were to teach the children to speak English properly and to break down the social animosities that existed between the Ukrainians and the larger Anglo-Saxon community beyond the school district.

A typical day at Moose Bay School began at nine o'clock. The students ranged in age from six to thirteen years. They walked to school each day, some of them coming as far as eight miles (weather permitting), since horses were too valuable to be used for the transportation of children. But they were all delighted to come, eager to learn their three R's, if only to escape the farm chores that were their usual lot. Unfortunately, none of them had managed to get beyond the fourth grade. Initially, Iser's largest problem was that he had also to teach them patriotic songs like "Rule Britannia" and "God Save the King" in the hope of turning them into loyal Canadians. Quite apart from their pro-German sympathies, Iser could not sing and was totally ignorant about music. Modern technology, however, came to his rescue: he prevailed upon Uncle Robert to send him up a second-hand gramophone with a big horn and a few records. So great was the novelty that the children were happy to sing along with whatever he played.

One incident which cannot be classed as scholastic happened quite early in the school year. Some of the boys indulged in the pastime of picking lice from the head of the boy in front of them and cracking them on their desks. This was a problem that had to be handled tactfully. Eventually Iser came up with a scheme that involved Mr. Strachan back in Winnipeg. Two cases of Lifebuoy soap were delivered to the school and each student given a bar to keep in his desk. One afternoon each week during the warm fall and spring weather, he simply marched the whole school down to the nearby lake. I think that these children would have loved the Lifebuoy song, had it been around then. In my mind's eye, I can picture my father, just a youth himself, on a warm afternoon in early June, waving a large bar of Lifebuoy over his head, leading a group of scraggly boys and giggling girls, like some latter-day Pied Piper, down the path, through the bushes and birches and down to the cool, clear waters, singing all the way: "Singing in the bathtub, Singing for joy, Singing the song of Lifebuoy, Can't help singing, 'Cause I know, Lifebuoy really stops B.O."

He could not order the students to jump into the lake and wash themselves thoroughly, but they put two and two together for themselves. The older girls took the younger ones out of sight along the lakeshore and instructed them to undress and scrub each other, hair and all. Iser stayed with the boys and saw to it that they did the same. In addition, he initiated a regular program of hand-washing in the schoolroom. Naturally enough, the children thoroughly enjoyed their afternoons with Lifebuoy at the lake. They loved the smell and when their teacher suggested that it would be a nice idea if they brought a fresh change of clothes with them to put on after their weekly wash, they happily agreed.

Mr. Hurtulak, a school trustee who watched over school expenditures very carefully, was very upset at what he regarded as a misappropriation of school funds.

"It's my fault," Iser freely admitted, "but if you wish to complain, you can write to Mr. Strachan in Winnipeg."

He did.

Another complaint was lodged by one of the former trustees, who protested that not only was the new teacher wasting their money on cases of soap but he was now wasting whole afternoons frolicking with the children in the lake . . . naked!

Other letters were sent to the Department of Education in Winnipeg demanding Iser's removal. Instead, Mr. Strachan wrote Iser a letter of congratulations, wishing him every success with his program of personal hygiene.

The school inspector reported that when he came on his official rounds, he found the young Russian Jewish school teacher and the Ukrainian Catholic farmers getting along very well. And that the anti-British feelings in the community seemed to have subsided. Indeed, several weeks before the federal election on December 17, 1917, one of the farmers came to ask Iser if he would teach the men how to write their names so that they could vote. Iser agreed to start night classes for those who were interested. The older men stayed at home but quite a few in their thirties and forties showed up. Each one practised his name assiduously and Mr. Hurtulak, the school trustee, was especially proud of his efforts in class.

When election day finally rolled around, polling booths were set up in the schoolhouse. Iser's duties combined many of the responsibilities of returning officer, polling clerk and scrutineer, as he attempted to make certain that only eligible voters cast ballots and that no one voted twice. Everything went smoothly until Mr. Hurtulak came to vote. Iser began to worry when he had not emerged from the booth after half an hour. Finally, he staggered forth, sweat pouring from his brow. "Well, I did it," he said proudly, displaying his signature where the X should have been. "Now, they'll know me in Ottawa!"

Iser returned to his studies at the University of Manitoba in 1919, when anti-Semitism in Winnipeg was particularly rife. And the University of Manitoba was not immune to this racist virus. One of Iser's fellow students took particular pleasure in making disparaging remarks about Jews during lab classes. Finally, Iser had it out with him. The next day, the lab instructor, a Scotsman who could not have failed to notice what had been building over the weeks, spotted the two black and blue faces. He asked each of them to stand up. After what seemed an eternity, he dryly observed, "It would appear that two of our colleagues have collided with the same streetcar." It was only then that Iser knew he would not be expelled over the incident.

Life as a medical student meant long hours of study, broken occasionally by parties given by other students, mainly the Jewish girls who were in Arts or at normal school. Iser was far too poor to give parties of his own, but as a prospective doctor he was very eligible for invitations. And because he was always hungry, he never turned one down no matter how plain his hostess might be. In fact, he found that the plainer the girl, the more food there was likely to be at the party.

Money was an eternal problem. There were no student loans in those days and scholarships were few and far between. Iser would work for Uncle Robert between terms to earn his tuition and occasionally Uncle Art would slip him a few dollars, but it was always touch and go financially. Every penny had to be counted, then counted again. Of course he was not alone in this. It was the common lot of most medical students and they learned to make do. Iser and a number of his medical school friends frequented the small cafes and coffee counters of North End Winnipeg, where they would order a bowl of soup for five cents. In those days, there was always a bottle of ketchup and a plate of bread or soda crackers on each table, so they would break up all the bread or crackers into their bowls of soup and pour the ketchup over it before digging in. Often, if the waitress was not the owner's wife or daughter, they'd ask for more bread or crackers. Naturally they had to move to other cafes when the proprietors caught on; there was no profit in a five-cent bowl of soup if they also had to supply a loaf of bread and a bottle of ketchup. After graduating from medical school and completing his internship, Iser never put ketchup on anything ever again.

Iser's parents did not attend the convocation ceremonies that marked his graduation from the University of Manitoba in 1924. Still exiled in Siberia, it is possible they didn't even know about them. But Uncles Robert and Art did. They sat proudly watching as the first member of the Steiman family ever to get a degree crossed the platform to receive his sheepskin from the Chancellor of the University. As to what the new doctor thought, he never told me. Manitoba, needless to say, had not turned out to be the "America" of Iser's early dreams. The Indians were on the reservations and the buffalo were nowhere to be seen and the streets of "New Jerusalem" definitely were not paved with gold — yet.

THE GENTLE EXILE

My grandfather, Solomon Steiman, was forty-nine-years-old when he waved goodbye to his fourteen-year-old son Iser in 1912. As he stood in the cold November wind watching the ship leave the Libau harbour, he must have worried. Had he made a wise choice for his son? It would be several weeks or more before he would even know if the boy had arrived safely. He could only pray. In the meantime he had work to do, customers to call on, a wife and other children to feed.

In the summer of 1914, Solomon took his wife Etza on a long-promised trip to Germany, where he placed his orders and arranged for the shipments of stock to be sent to him from the Böker factory in Solingen, near Dusseldorf, for the winter ahead. They were in Berlin when Archduke Franz Ferdinand and his wife Sophie were assassinated at Sarajevo on June 28. They returned to Dvinsk on July 30, the day Russia ordered general mobilization. At 7:00 p.m. the next day, Germany declared war on Russia.

Early on in the war, which most thought would be over in three months, the Russian army suffered a major defeat at Tannenburg (August 26-30) and another at the Battle of the Masurian Lakes (September 6-15), between which the Germans took nearly 250,000 Russian prisoners. As military disaster followed military disaster, it was not long before a scapegoat had to be found for the abysmal performance of the Russian army. As was customary in this part of the world, the Jews were selected. They were charged with harbouring pro-German sympathies and spying for the enemy. A popular Russian cartoon showed a Jew and a German shaking hands — and the Jew filling his pockets with German marks.

Solomon Steiman, it seemed to the Dvinsk police, fitted the picture to a T, despite the fact that his son Mark, at age fourteen, had just been conscripted into the Russian army. One evening in November or December of 1914, Solomon was taken from his home and led away to the police station where he and about twenty other Jews were charged with spying for Germany. At one in the morning they were transferred to the headquarters of the political police in Officers Street where they were imprisoned in a basement room previously used to store potatoes. The nineteenth century social revolutionary and philosopher, A.I. Herzen, observed that "so terrible is the confusion, brutality and arbitrariness and corruption of Russian justice and of the Russian police that a man of humbler class who falls into the hands of the law is more afraid of the process of the law itself than of any legal punishment. He looks forward with impatience to the time when he will be sent to Siberia; his martyrdom ends with the beginning of his punishment."

Perhaps then it was with a great deal of relief that Solomon greeted his banishment by administrative decree, rather than being sent over to trial. Exile he could deal with and possibly survive, but jail he could not. Besides there were others who would be going with him. It was Etza and the children he worried about. Solomon's group of politicals was destined for Viatka in the Urals, 450 miles north-east of Moscow. The exact route they took is unknown, as are how many weeks or months they were in transit. Suffice it to say Solomon must have been hardy to survive, rattling along in filthy prison boxcars (called Stolypins after the Prime Minister), bumping for days in wagons and carts, walking for miles and miles in all kinds of weather, probably in the company of hardened criminals and cut-throats.

Although Viatka had been a staging point in early trade routes across the northern Urals, it remained a typical old Russian provincial city of about 25,000. Centred on the ancient Uspienski Cathedral of the Trifon Monastery, there was little else to distinguish it physically, apart from a few grand residences in the unique Russian classical style of the eighteenth century — a jail, a hospital, a theatre, a library, a museum and a cinema. It was famous for its Dymkova wooden toys and had some leather, fur, lumber and metalworking industries. Because it was surrounded by an impenetrable, swampy forest of pine, fir, spruce and birch, escape from this remote town was almost impossible — making it an ideal place of exile. Indeed, it had been used by the Tsars for the last hundred years for that very purpose. As it was beyond the Pale of Settlement, Solomon was surprised to find about four hundred Jews living in the city and its environs and not all of them exiles. There was even a small synagogue which had been legalized in 1896 by order of the Minister of the Interior.

Apparently, it was up to Solomon and his fellow exiles to earn such living as they could in Viatka. Solomon was a man of commerce. In Dvinsk, he had lived well. He had put money away and if the situation allowed, Etza could send a little to Viatka every month. But he was worried more about his family than himself. He still had some of the money he had taken for the journey from Dvinsk, as well as some of the Böker cutlery, scissors and other instruments Etza had packed for the purposes of sale or barter. His clothing was adequate for Viatka's sub-arctic temperatures and he was able to find room and board with the family of a Jewish exile who had settled there the year before. He quickly posted a letter to Etza assuring her he was well and settling in.

Meanwhile the war was going from bad to worse. The Russian army continued to suffer even more disastrous defeats. On April 28, 1915 at the time of the religious festival of Shavuos, an edict was issued ordering that all Lithuanian Jews be evacuated from the Pale of Settlement within twenty-four hours. This was the beginning of the forced removal of all Jews from their historic homelands within the Russian Empire to prevent their collaboration with the advancing German armies. The pattern established in Lithuania soon would be applied to Latvia. All Jews were to be at the railway stations in their villages, towns and cities at a designated time. Trains were to be provided free of charge to the evacuees and Russian peasants were paid to transport Jews from remote villages to the awaiting trains. The old, young, men, women and children hastily gathered up whatever they could carry — what they left behind would be treated as booty to be fought over by their former Russian neighbours. Crammed into boxcars, they were transported en masse from the war zone.

Etza was attending Shavuos service when the rabbi announced that a trainload of Lithuanian Jews, desperately in need of tea, milk and medical aid, had arrived at Petersburg Station. All the congregants rushed to their aid. Etza and the two older girls ran home to collect such food as they had on hand. Little were they prepared, however, for the sight that greeted them at the station: eighty open freight cars filled to the brim with weary, miserable refugees. A committee was quickly formed to supervise the distribution of food. The young Jewish girls hauled in water to wash down the filthy boxcars. Two doctors arrived from the Jewish hospital and Etza helped one of them vaccinate hundreds of children. Unfortunately, despite the pleas of Dvinsk's Jewish leaders that the train at least be allowed to stay over until the next day, by midnight it was on its way to Kreslavka, Polotsk, Vitebsk and finally to Mogilev in the Ukraine, where most of the refugees were to be resettled.

The evacuation of the Lithuanian Jews, however, was not followed by the expected Russian victory. In fact, the Germans were advancing towards Dvinsk. One day Etza looked up and saw an airplane in the distant sky. It was a sight followed by the sounds of great explosions, much louder than she had ever imagined possible. Bombs landed on Dvinsk's Petersburg railway station and on the fortress. Then in late September, 1915, on the eve of Rosh Hashanah, a bomb landed in the middle of the marketplace, killing five people and wounding another forty. By this time, Etza was beginning to despair that she and the children would ever be evacuated from Dvinsk. When the trains finally began to arrive, she decided to gather up what they could and try to find their way to Solomon in Viatka.

She and Lily packed up the necessities, including the remaining stock of Böker cutlery, and, loaded down with bundles and bags, the four of them made their way to the Petersburg station. Etza, now forty and Lily, twenty, carried most everything between them. Ten-year-old Dora was charged with carrying Bronya, who was four. The streets were filled with their friends and neighbours also fleeing for their lives, pushing and pulling all kinds of carts, wagons, and wheelbarrows loaded to capacity with household goods and prized possessions, most of which would be abandoned along the road.

At the station, it took many hours before they were able to claim a place in a freight car headed south in the direction of Mogilev, which is hardly en route to Viatka. Little did Etza know that it would be months before they would be able to proceed beyond that point, by which time the Russian Revolution would have erupted, adding chaos to calamity throughout the land. Of that last, long leg of their horrendous journey, they spoke little in later years. The hunger, cold, fatigue, the endless waiting at stations and sidings, the bribing of stationmasters for space in a box car, the greasing of palms of greedy *balagulas* (cart-drivers), the walking and walking and walking.

When they finally found Solomon a year or so later, he was baking bread. A man who had been waited on hand and foot all his life, as was the custom, was baking bread! Looking for Solomon's address, they had trudged along the dusty street peering into windows until finally they saw a stocky little man with a moustache, goatee and thick, steamed-over glasses hauling loaves of bread out of the clay and brick oven with a long flat wooden spatula. But what a reunion it must have been!

One can only imagine the tears of joy, the hugs, the kisses, everyone talking at once. Then —

"Oy vay, what's burning?"

"THE BREAD."

Reunited, the Steimans had to settle into accommodations shared with another family. Lily and Dora found work, Lily in the department of records in the municipal hall where A.I. Herzen had spent so many dreary hours. Because she was a fine artist, she was able to earn extra money doing charcoal and pencil portraits. As she recalled this many years later: "People came to me with photographs of their children, their loved ones, their departed, and I would copy them onto large sheets of thick white paper, which was very expensive. I then sprayed them with a fixative. Customers would have to leave a deposit and in charging them I had to take into consideration the fluctuations of the ruble, which was very unstable at the time." Dora, having won a prize for penmanship in school in Dvinsk, found employment in the local theatre copying out scripts. (Years later in Winnipeg, Lily would become a much-sought-after antique restorer and Dora a caterer of distinction — eventually, no Jewish wedding in Canada was worth talking about unless several of Dora's chocolate tortes had been flown in from Winnipeg.) Bronya, of course, was enrolled in one of the local schools.

With Dora and Lily bringing in a few rubles and Solomon scraping up whatever he could, they just managed. After the Bolshevik government came into power in November 1917, ration cards were issued, but often there was no food to be had. In 1918, Etza gave birth to yet another child, a boy they named Boris. Food was so scarce that after Boris was weaned, Etza fed him mainly on potatoes. He was a hardy little fellow and survived. But the next child, a girl, Masha, born in 1920, was weak and sickly and needed a lot of attention. Fortunately, Viatka was sufficiently far from the civil war that raged between the Whites and the Reds between 1918 and 1920 so that the Steimans were spared the worst of that particular horror. However, they did not escape the effects of the famine of 1921. Dora had become friendly with a couple of Russian girls and occasionally they would get into a sleigh, drive across the frozen lake to a farm and come back late at night, tired and cold, with some potatoes, chicken, milk, eggs and butter. But as Lily recalled many years later, "They could not go to that farm very often. It was too dangerous. It was against the law, of course, but when hunger knocks at your door you find courage and strength."

All three girls made friends quickly amongst the other exiled Jewish families. They went to the theatre or movies when they had saved up a few kopecks. More often, they met at each other's homes to listen to the gramophone or sing around the piano. Etza and Solomon also gradually made friends and on Saturday mornings they would go to the little synagogue, just a short walk from their house, where they found particular comfort.

In the meantime, Mark, who had miraculously survived the war, was demobilized in early 1918 and made his way to Viatka. Very little is known

Mark Steiman, somewhere on the Eastern Front, Russia, 1917

about Mark's three-and-one-half years in the Tsarist army, except that it was during the last bitter year of the war that Mark came down with pneumonia that left him with permanently weak lungs. That he survived at all was miraculous considering the indescribable hardships the ordinary Russian soldier had to endure. We do have a photograph of him taken somewhere at the front in the summer of 1917. In it he sports a slim moustache, grown no doubt in an effort to appear older than his seventeen years and his high-necked, summer-weight tunic with its lowslung belt clings to his sweaty chest.

He has just pushed back his cap and wiped the sweat from his face. But he's missed the smudge on his right cheek. He nevertheless looks disarmingly handsome in his uniform, quite the lady-killer.

The train Mark boarded en route from Moscow to Viatka was to prove more fateful than the war itself in Mark's life. The third class "hard" car, crammed with soldiers, a lot of them wounded, was hot, stuffy and smelled of that characteristically Russian blend of leather boots, black bread, garlic, cabbage and *makhorka* (tobacco). Mark found a place among a group of young nurses also returning from the front and before long he took out his guitar and started to play. Vodka miraculously appeared and one can imagine his clear tenor voice rising above the click-clacking of the carriage wheels and the coarse laughter of the soldiers.

At Nizhny-Novgorod (later to be renamed Gorky) several of the nurses got off. Among them was the one Mark had taken a shine to. She was older than the others, with dark hair and eyes. She had a pouting mouth and her photographs portray a certain sternness. But she appealed to Mark enough for him to ask one of her friends for her name and address. Perhaps some day he'd meet her again, he thought. But for the time being he had to get to Viatka, to the family. He had to get well again and find some kind of work. Certainly, he was in no position to think of marriage. Faina Frierman, however, was never to be far from his mind and when he landed a job as a book-keeper with a confectioner in Viatka he wrote to her. Yes, she remembered the good-looking soldier in the train who played the guitar and sang. Yes, he could come to visit one day. Mark decided to take the plunge. He went to Nizhny-Novgorod to woo and win the fair Faina.

The family was aghast. From their point of view, Faina Frierman, when they found out about her, had at least four strikes against her. One, she was eight or ten years older than Mark: a brazen hussy who had seduced him away from his family. Two, she lived in Nizhny-Novgorod and would probably make his life miserable until he moved there. Three, she was very poor, and domineering to boot. And four, Solomon and Etza had already selected Mark's bride. But Mark didn't seem to find anything objectionable at all about Faina and they were married in May, 1920. In 1921, their daughter (my cousin) Mara was born — the first of Solomon and Etza Steiman's grandchildren.

Prior to 1921 and Lenin's New Economic Policy, which encouraged

Mark and Faina Steiman, Viatka, USSR, 1923

temporarily private business, there were frequent changes in Bolshevik policy and methods, at least in Viatka. Just as the Jewish population began adjusting to one new policy, another replaced it. The promulgation of the Soviet Constitution in 1918, which disenfranchised the so-called "non-toiling classes," was a hard blow to petty businessmen like Solomon who now found themselves classified as "socially undesirable." He found making a living increasingly difficult in consequence.

Late one evening in September 1920, after a particularly unsuccessful day, Solomon came home leading a small pig that he had exchanged for his last pair of Böker scissors. As it was too late to barter it for something else, he brought it home, intending to keep it in the backyard overnight. When Etza saw him in the street with a pig on a rope, she flew into a rage and told him to get rid of it. No matter how hard things were with them, she was not going to have anything *trayf* (not kosher) anywhere near her children. Solomon turned around and took the pig to a neighbour in the next street, a gentile, who agreed to keep it overnight — for a price.

The following evening after dinner, with Lily settled in a corner busy with a charcoal portrait, Bronya rocking Masha to sleep, Dora copying a play,

Boris playing at her feet and Solomon and Etza sipping the last of the tea in their glasses, there was a loud knock on the door. Bronya ran for it. A tall thin man in a black leather coat and a small peaked hat, accompanied by a burly companion similarly dressed, pushed their way past her, demanding the whereabouts of Solomon. They identified themselves as members of the dread Cheka, the Soviet secret police. It soon became apparent that someone had informed "the comrades" that Solomon had been speculating. The thin man accused him of profiteering. They'd been watching him for some time and now they had proof. Didn't he know there had been a revolution? The new people's government was in the process of changing the old ways. He motioned to his cohort to start searching. Together they emptied drawers, opened boxes and cupboards but found nothing. The heavyset man then looked at the cradle and said, "These wily Jews don't fool me." He dumped Masha onto the floor and began to rummage through her blankets. Bronya had lunged to catch the baby, but couldn't reach her in time. Masha hit the floor with a soft thud and started shrieking. Solomon was carted off for further questioning. Masha was to die before morning.

Etza and the girls were grief-stricken. "Why can't the doctor fix the baby?" "Who could have informed on Papa?"

Every morning Etza prepared a bundle of kosher food for Solomon, which she or Bronya would carry to the prison on the other side of town. The prison, however, was filthy and it wasn't long before Solomon fell ill. As the weeks and months passed and his condition worsened, Etza and the girls feared he would die. They went before the revolutionary council to try to persuade it to let Solomon go. But only when the local Bolshevik authorities were sure he was dying did they magnanimously set him free. They had not reckoned with the restorative powers of Etza's chicken soup!

"What a country! How was one to live in such a place?" Enter Lily. Stage centre. Lily, the eldest, diminutive, full-breasted and bird-like, not even five feet tall, rose to the occasion. While Solomon had been in prison, Lily looked through all his papers and found Robert Steiman's address in Winnipeg and without telling her parents, wrote him of their terrible plight.

Unbeknownst to Lily and coincidental with her campaign to get the rest of the Steiman family to Canada, a delegation sponsored by the Canadian Alliance of Ukrainian Jews for the Relief of Pogrom Victims arrived in the USSR to deliver relief supplies and to render every possible assistance to relatives of Canadian Jews desiring to emigrate to Canada. After long and serious negotiations with the Jewish section of the People's Commissariat for National Minorities, the Soviets finally allowed the families of British, Canadian or American citizens to emigrate. Travelling expenses would have to be covered by the relatives or ethnic organizations abroad. But to set up the machinery to handle the immigration to Canada, England or the United States was no easy matter. It was necessary to obtain from one of the border countries a permit for the temporary admission of Jewish emigrants from Soviet Russia, where they would be able to contact the immigration officials of the English-speaking countries, receive money for transportation expenses and so on. Such arrangements could not be made in Moscow. It was necessary to go to either Tallinn, Riga or Kovno. By the middle of 1921, all Jewish organizations, both in America and in Europe, were vitally concerned with the emigration problem. At a conference in Prague called by the Hebrew Immigration Aid Society of America and the Executive Committee of the Jewish World Relief, an organization called Emigdirect was created with headquarters in Berlin. On September 17, 1922, Emigdirect signed a protocol with the Lithuanian and Latvian governments in which the latter agreed to grant visas to transmigrants leaving Russia and to allow them temporary residence in their countries until they received permits or visas enabling them to proceed further.

From then on, Riga became the main centre for Russian transmigrants. Legal immigration from Soviet Russia continued for almost a decade and helped to realize one of the main purposes of the Canadian Alliance of Ukrainian Jews — the uniting of families. While the final arrangements for transmigrants were made by European organizations, it is an historical fact that the representatives of Canadian Jewish organizations were the first to open negotiations with the authorities in Soviet Russia for legal emigration from that country. The USSR apparently was more amenable to dealing with the Canadians, since the Brits and Yanks had more actively supported the counter-revolutionaries.

Robert, the elder statesman of the Steiman family, found out that Solomon's family could get into Canada as farmers destined for the Jewish agricultural colony, New Hirsch, at Camper in the Interlake district of Manitoba. He answered Lily's letter with what was becoming a universal panacea: "Come to Canada."

Lily wrote letters, waited interminably in dingy offices, filled in endless forms and travelled back and forth to Moscow. Finally their passports, worth more than gold, were issued in March 1923.

With permission to leave Viatka, they packed up their few belongings, including the samovar and whatever cutlery was left (a few knives and forks so sharp they could kill) and started their westward journey. En route to Riga, they stopped in

Etza Steiman's Soviet passport, with photos of Brownie and Boris, stamped by Canadian Immigration, January 7, 1924

Dvinsk for a few days. By then most of the Jews who had been exiled or forcibly evacuated during the Great War had returned and were once again playing an important role in the life of the city — something they would continue to do until 1941, when they would all be exterminated by the Germans. After a last look at their former home now filled with strangers, there was nothing more for them to do but move on.

By the middle of December their transit certificates and tickets were in

Etza and Solomon Steiman, with Boris, Lily, Dora and Brownie, Winnipeg, 1924

their hands. On January 7, 1924, they boarded a ship of the Hamburg Line bound for New York. Not a minute too soon. Later that same month, January 24 to be exact, Lenin died. Who knew what would happen next, except that it could be nothing good.

When their train finally pulled into the CPR station in Winnipeg, there on the platform were all the Steimans who had come to Canada before them. Robert and Sarah and their children, Mendel with his long white beard and his beloved Hannah Zelda, Max the Busy Bee and Rosie and their seven children, George the *luftmensh*, and Art the laughing bachelor. Standing a little apart from the group was a handsome young man at whom Solomon peered through his thick glasses before embracing. His fourteen-year-old son Iser was now twenty-six and a doctor of medicine.

C O U N T R Y D O C T O R

With degree in hand and his internship behind him, it was Iser's ambition to apply his hard-won medical skills where they were most needed. Moose Bay he could live without but he knew that he could find a fulfilling career in some other, if slightly less primitive, rural community in need of a doctor. Of course, he could not have afforded to buy into one of the established city practices, even if he had wanted to. Hospital appointments in Winnipeg were also out of the question, given the quota system. And he did not want to become an ambulance chaser in search of patients, which was the sad fate of a number of young Jewish doctors he knew. He, however, did want the option of practising outside Manitoba. But in order to accomplish this, he first had to take the Medical Council of Canada written and oral examinations. He had no worries about passing. It was the cost — a monumental $250.

Iser Steiman, the eligible young doctor, Winnipeg, 1924

As he surveyed his prospective sources of credit, things seemed pretty bleak. Uncle Robert had the money but, as Iser had long since discovered, he made it a practice never to help those who could be reasonably expected to help themselves. Uncle Max the Busy Bee was bankrupt. Uncle George was in Chicago, doing no one knew what. Uncle Art would lend it to him if only he had it. His father was in absolutely dire straits in Viatka. Who else? Grandfather Mendel had no money to speak of. His aunts? . . . Well . . . Aunt Sara had always encouraged him in his studies and her husband Haim, both uncle by marriage and second cousin to Iser, seemed to be making a lot of money in partnership with his brother, Herschel Leib, in the Dominion Garment Factory . . . And the word among the family was that Uncle Haim contributed to religious schools and other special charities. Iser didn't want to ask him, but after long deliberation finally decided he had no choice in the matter.

"No," Uncle Haim said flatly. He would not consider it. That Iser was now a doctor and could reasonably be expected to repay the money didn't matter. His refusal was based on the fact that Iser was not as religious as Uncle Haim would have liked and that it would have damaged his reputation to help what Haim described as a non-practising Jew.

It was late morning when Iser left the shabby Dominion Garment Factory premises at 577 Selkirk Avenue. He was very disappointed. Walking along, wondering perhaps what his future would be practicing in Moose Bay, he stopped in front of an apothecary shop run by an old friend of his, a Russian Jew named Bloch.

Bloch waived Iser in and regarding him briefly through his pince-nez, asked in Russian, "What is the matter with you? You who have just reached the apex of success, you should be floating on a cloud. Why are you looking so desperate?"

"I've got nothing to look forward to."

"Nonsense! In Russia, doctors were gods. I know it's not quite the same in this country, but still . . . What more could you ask?"

Iser explained that he wanted to leave Winnipeg, maybe to practice in Saskatchewan or Ontario.

"So? Something is stopping you?"

"Just one little thing. The two hundred and fifty dollar registration fee for the Canadian Medical Council examination. For me this is insurmountable."

"Insurmountable?"

"My family either won't or can't lend it to me and I have no security to offer the bank."

"Well, I cannot lend it to you either but I can buy you a good lunch to cheer you up."

Leaving Bloch's assistant to run the shop, they continued down Selkirk towards their destination, a restaurant on Main Street. However, when they reached the bank building at the corner of Salter Street, Bloch said, "I hope you don't mind waiting here for a moment. I have a little bit of business inside with my friend, Dr. Pearlman. I want him to join us for lunch." Dr. Pearlman's office was on the second floor above the bank. An old-country physician of excellent reputation, Isaac Pearlman had been a *feldscher* in Russia before emigrating. In Winnipeg, he not only ran a successful private practice but was a lecturer with the department of physiology at the University of Manitoba.

As Iser waited on the corner enjoying the sunshine and the passing scene, he thought, "Thank God I'm not like Uncle Haim. He would never understand that it is fortune enough for one day to have lunch with two such intelligent and distinguished-looking men."

After perhaps twenty minutes, Bloch and Pearlman appeared. They asked Iser to come into the bank with them where, to his utter amazement (and eternal gratitude), Iser discovered that a demand loan for two hundred and fifty dollars had been arranged for him. Dr. Pearlman, at Bloch's behest, had signed as his guarantor.

Money in hand, Iser had no problem with the Canadian Medical Council examinations. His new life as a doctor was about to begin. All he needed now was a physician's bag, a set of instruments, some basic medical supplies and a location for his shingle. Obtaining these necessities proved easier than expected. Another friend of Iser's, Claude Hyman, ran a medical supply house. When he went to see him, Claude smiled. "Well, Iser, I guess it's time for us to do business!"

"Claude, I'd be happy to do business, but I don't have any money."

"That's no obstacle. Pay when you start to earn."

It was next a question of finding a suitable location to set up practice. Word had already spread via the Jewish telegraph that he wanted to set up a rural practice and he soon received a call from a man who ran a grain elevator at Benito, Manitoba. This was a small town on the Manitoba-Saskatchewan border, about twenty-five miles south-west of Swan River (and about twenty miles east of Pelly). They wanted another doctor — a Jewish doctor.

It was an early summer's evening when he stepped off the Canadian National Railway coach at Benito, where he was met by the elevator operator and several of the man's friends, all of them anxious to have Iser set up practice in town. On their advice, he rented a room above the Chinese restaurant, the only restaurant in town. He slept well that night, but in the morning his spirits were somewhat dampened by the fact that it was raining and he had only two dollars left in his pocket. As protocol required, he presented himself to meet the town's established doctor, Dr. Baldwin, a man now in his seventies. Iser told Dr. Baldwin that he had been made very much aware of the esteem in which the older physician was held by everyone in the district but he had been invited to Benito by people who believed there was so much work in the area, that there was plenty for two doctors.

Doctor Baldwin dryly assured him he had no objection to Iser setting up his practice in Benito. "After all, you're a licenced doctor, you can practice anywhere you wish. What objections could I possibly have?" He then asked if Iser had rented an office yet. Iser told him he hadn't since he had arrived in town only the evening before, but had been assured that the former tailor's shop on the main street was available.

Later that morning, Iser's new friend from the elevator took him to meet Max Laimon, owner of the Benito general store, who was delighted to hear that a new doctor was coming to town. He was pleased, not only because Iser was Jewish, but also because a large portion of the population thereabouts was Doukhobor and German and Iser could speak their languages. It was while he was talking to Laimon that the call came through that there was a medical emergency at nearby Thunder Hill. The elevator operator drove Iser out in his Model-T Ford over a road now perilously slippery from the heavy rain, its crater-like potholes brimming with gumbo. With some trepidation, Iser, carrying his brand-new medical bag, entered the communal Doukhobor house. His first patient was a middle-aged, Russian-speaking woman. He made his diagnosis, wrote out his first prescription, filled it on the spot and collected his first fee (enough to see him through the next few days).

Feeling assured of the future, Iser returned to Winnipeg the next day to gather up his personal belongings and to obtain medical supplies. Two days later he was back in Benito, only to find that Dr. Baldwin had seen to it that the tailor's shop had been rented, as well as every other previously available accommodation, except for his bedroom over the Chinese restaurant.

Patients, however, were already lining up to consult the new young doctor. A storekeeper, who was beyond the influence of Dr. Baldwin and the other town worthies, came to his rescue by offering, for fifteen dollars a month, a room above his store. Iser was more than delighted and immediately set to work, using an ordinary kitchen table for examinations. Occasionally, his friendly elevator operator drove him out to make house calls; otherwise, he used the services of the drayman. The fee for house calls was a dollar a mile, so he did very well.

He had only been in Benito a month when the two Jewish merchants in Aaron, just across the Saskatchewan border and a whistle stop away along the CNR branch line, found out that Iser was in the area. They convinced him to set up office there one or two days a week, the town not being large enough to support a full-time doctor. Iser arranged to rent a small back room in the post office for ten dollars a month.

In the late fall of 1924, he was able to purchase an ancient Model-A Ford, complete with struts and side curtains. The gas tank was under the

Drs. Steiman (standing centre) and Baldwin
(seated) and friends, Benito, Manitoba, 1924

windshield and the gasoline reached the carburetor by a gravity-feed. It served him well except when he had to go up the steep hill on the other side of the Swan River. Then he had to back up the hill to keep the carburetor from being starved for fuel. He also allowed himself the small luxury of a Kodak box camera. As he tootled along the bumpy roads he would stop now and then to capture an incomparable prairie scene. On calls to remote farms, he photographed his patients — an old Ukranian woman spinning, a work-worn mother standing with her child at the door of a thatched cottage, a farmer carrying a pail, a woman leading the cows home. There was time in those days — time to sit down with his patient's family, to enjoy a bowl of borscht with freshly baked bread, to talk, to take a picture or two. Back in town, he would develop the film in his darkened office with chemicals he mixed himself.

Shortly after acquiring the car, Iser moved his main office from Benito to Pelly, some ten miles west of Aaron. He continued to make himself available in his Aaron office on Mondays and Thursdays. He was happy to leave Benito. He had never been able to overcome his distaste for Dr. Baldwin and his cohorts, whose influence pervaded the town like miasma. It may also have been that Iser now saw his medical future in Saskatchewan rather than in Manitoba.

Iser Steiman and friend in front of his office, Pelly, 1925

Whenever he could find the time, he would travel to Winnipeg to make certain his parents, sisters and younger brother were settling into their new lives without undue difficulty. (The New Hirsch Jewish agricultural colony, founded in 1911, had foundered just before their arrival.) Catching the local from Pelly to Canora or Swan River, where he had to change trains, entailed a trip that took all night and part of the next morning. But given his medical responsibilities, he could never stay more than a couple of days at a time. Besides, he was not so wealthy that he could afford to miss one of the maternity cases for which he was paid twenty-five dollars (that is, if he were paid at all).

In his parents' home on Dufferin Avenue, Iser was always a celebrity. Etza enjoyed fussing over him, cooking all his favourite Russian and Jewish delicacies, like Carrot Tzimmes — a simple enough dish that has remained one of my personal favourites:

CARROT TZIMMES

8 large carrots (about 2 pounds) pared and sliced into thick rounds
4 tablespoons vegetable oil or butter

1/2 cup liquid honey	*1 teaspoon grated lemon rind*
1/3 cup brown sugar	*1/2 teaspoon salt*
1/4 teaspoon ground ginger	*1/2 cup pitted prunes*

Parboil carrots in salted water for ten minutes. Drain. Add honey, sugar, oil or butter and prunes. Bake uncovered in low oven stirring occasionally until carrots are tender and richly glazed, about 20 minutes. Stir in lemon rind and ginger. Serve as accompaniment to meat dish. Serves six.

After supper Solomon brings his accounts to the dining table to go over them with Iser. He's worried about expenses. Iser tells him not to worry; he'll help. They discuss family problems. Boris's tonsils are inflamed and swollen. Iser removes them on the spot and sends him up to bed. Bronya (now called Brownie), who has a beautiful singing voice, wants to join the Winnipeg mixed choir.

"So let her," Iser advises.

"It's full of *goyim* (gentiles)," Solomon objects.

"She can't spend every minute of her life in North End Winnipeg."

"But she's so young."

"She's had good parents. You've taught her well. Besides, Papa, it's 1925 and this is Canada — not Dvinsk or Viatka."

"Now that Lily's finally getting married, what about Dora? It's time to think about a husband for Dora. You had better meet this Myer Zaslovsky who has been coming around. And talking about weddings, what about that nice girl, Esther? Mama and I were talking to her parents . . . "

"Papa, I have other things to think about. We'll talk about Esther some other time."

Social life in the North End of Winnipeg in the 1920s was lively, but restrictive. Everyone knew everyone else, or was related in some way. There was a never-ending round of bar mitzvahs, weddings and funerals, each with its attendant party. There was also a lot of coming and going, backing and forthing between Winnipeg and the small towns of Manitoba, Saskatchewan and the border States to the south, where Jews formed a large percentage of the merchant and professional classes. In most of the little towns along the CP and CN Railway lines, one could be sure of finding a Jewish doctor, lawyer or dentist and a storekeeper or two or three, depending on the size or importance of the town. They sent their young boys to Winnipeg to study. Young girls were sent to visit, to shop and, often, to catch a husband. A few Jewish girls went to university but more went into teaching. With Grade 11 and a year at normal school, they could get jobs in elementary schools anywhere in the province and be considered "educated professionals."

This group of aspiring young female teachers, with marriage in mind, had no end of parties to which they invited the young law and medical students. My father's family had become friendly with Esther's. They exchanged visits and the mamas, as Jewish mamas are wont to do all over the world, thought: "Wouldn't it be wonderful if my Esther and your Iser . . . " Poor Iser. Poor Esther.

At the time, Esther was teaching at Winnipeg's Norquay Elementary School. According to one of her former female colleagues, she was short, plump and sweet: a young woman with a sunny disposition. At the age of twenty-three, Esther was looking forward to her forthcoming marriage to a storekeeper from Grand Forks, North Dakota, who was crazy about her.

Unquestionably, Iser was a catch. Good-looking, with irresistible dark brown eyes and curly black hair, and a doctor to boot! A lot of young women (and some not so young) were after him. Esther, with a little help from the mamas and the blessings of both families, pushed herself to the head of the queue. She broke off her engagement and set her cap for my father-to-be. Iser was flattered, and more. To my knowledge, he had not previously had a serious love affair in all of his twenty-six years (there are questions a good Jewish daughter of my generation could not even consider asking her father). As to how serious Iser was about Esther . . . my Aunt Ida remembered seeing a framed photo of her displayed in his office in Pelly. Certainly, Esther considered that they had made a match.

In the wilds of east-central Saskatchewan, also known as Pelly, a framed photo of a Winnipeg sweetheart was no defence against a determined Jewish mama who considered Iser the rightful property of one or other of her daughters. Obviously, a single man of Jewish descent in possession of a medical degree must be in want of a proper wife. So when my father arrived with a borrowed suitcase, a bag of instruments and a pocketful of debts, he was welcomed by all the Jewish mamas in the neighbourhood and, in particular, Ida Shatsky, who made his well-being her pet project. Iser had rented a little house across the road from the Shatsky Bros. General Store as a combination office and home. Auntie Ida cleaned it. She painted its interior. She found him a second-hand couch, a table, chairs and whatever else was necessary to make the place comfortable. When she saw that the interior of his old Model-A was a mess, the springs bursting through the seats, she tied them down and reupholstered the seats with the darkest-coloured oilcloth that the Shatsky brothers stocked in their store. She regularly invited Iser to dinner, or would cook extra portions of whatever she and Uncle Morris were having and deliver them to his door. Iser had Melting Moments coming out his ears! Why? She and Morris had three daughters, the eldest being the blond, doll-faced, highly eligible Bessie (not to be confused with Big Auntie Bessie) — my mother Laura's cousin and best friend.

Iser was also a frequent guest at the home of Elizabeth and Samuel Shatsky. Aunt Ida would have been furious if she'd known that he thought the other Mrs. Shatsky the sweetest, most charming woman he had ever met. Of course, Grandmother Elizabeth was not doing any Jewish mama *shtik* (act). She knew that her eldest daughter, Laura, who was visiting in Vancouver at the time Iser moved to Pelly, would never be pressured into any old-country-type arranged marriage. Laura was a thoroughly modern, New World woman, who would make up her own mind about such matters. In the meantime, Iser got to know Laura's two brothers, Lawrence and a small devil of a boy named Harold, as well as baby Shannon. By the time Laura came home from her holiday, Iser had become something of a fixture in both Shatsky households.

As it happened, Iser was at the station to pick up medical supplies when the train bearing his destiny rolled in and an attractive young woman, fashionably flapperish, alighted. Although at this time he was in no financial position to even consider marriage, he couldn't help being attracted to Laura, thrown together as they were at Sabbath dinners and evenings spent around the piano.

The respective fathers of the two beautiful cousins, Sam and Morris Shatsky, knew everyone in the district and were extremely helpful to the young doctor in getting his new practice established. In fact, Iser's practice was becoming quite brisk. He did minor surgery in his own office. It was not well-equipped but no one complained, because the nearest hospital was thirty-five miles away at Canora and the roads were impassable most of the year. Sometimes he scheduled tonsil clinics in the town's community hall. Ten or fifteen children from distant farms would be brought in by their parents, and the nurse from Benito would come into town to administer the anaesthetic.

One morning, having scheduled a clinic, he was horrified to learn at the last moment that the nurse from Benito was not coming. With patients already on their way by horse and wagon from distant farms, there was no way to cancel it. When Laura heard of his plight, she volunteered, willing to learn by doing. "You're not squeamish, are you?" he asked doubtfully.

"Not a bit," she laughed. "Have you seen what they do to cows and pigs around here?"

Iser showed her precisely how to administer the anaesthetic. The two of them worked well together. Laura was tremendously impressed with him, especially his manner with the children, for when the young patients "came to" on mattresses spread on the floor, he pressed sugar candies into their hands. As for Iser, by the end of that long day's tonsil clinic, he was convinced that Laura was an extraordinary young woman who would make an excellent doctor's wife. And it was not long after that he realized he had fallen in love, not only with the prairies, but also irrefutably with a prairie girl.

Meanwhile, back in Winnipeg, Esther was pouring out her heart in letters to Iser and receiving, as time went on, less-than-enthusiastic replies. She became desperate. Bouts of hysteria replaced her happy personality. She lost weight. She had to take time off from teaching. Her parents couldn't understand what was going on. Neither could Iser's. Of course, he had not confided in them that he had fallen in love with Laura Shatsky. For their part, Solomon and Etza had never had the nerve to inform their son that they had been planning his future with Esther's parents — to the point where they virtually had concluded a contract for the union of their respective children. In a last-ditch attempt to secure her future, Esther decided to spend New Year's 1926 with the Brounstein family, relatives who farmed near Pelly. Too late. Iser made their "break" final in Winnipeg a month or so later, with the help of Uncles Robert and Art. It was Art who escorted Esther to Robert's home on Selkirk Avenue, where Iser was waiting with Robert. A few minutes later, Art led the weeping woman away.

No one knows exactly what Iser told Esther. However, when Laura and Iser fixed their wedding date for March 16, 1926, the collective wail of Esther's family could be heard for hundreds of miles. Of course Esther was broken-hearted, but her second broken engagement would no doubt have slipped into obscurity had she not had an uncle with a law degree. Her lawyer uncle, a Reform Jew from England, dragged up some mouldering fifteenth-century common-law practice and convinced her parents that they could take Iser for a bundle by suing for breach of promise.

Even though the case was pending, Laura and Iser decided to marry. Ordinarily, any Steiman or Shatsky marriage would have taken place in Winnipeg, no matter where the bride and groom actually lived. But under the circumstances, Iser and Laura decided to have their wedding in Pelly. March is traditionally a frightful month in Saskatchewan and 1926 was no exception. But for this wedding everyone came. By train. By car. By horse and cutter.

The houses of relatives and friends were filled to bursting. There were people sleeping everywhere — even in Iser's office — so that on their wedding night Laura and Iser had to sleep apart. There would be no honeymoon. They couldn't afford one. But even if they had had the money, nobody could have escaped Pelly the night of March 16th. Winter had returned with a vengeance.

The case of the breach of promise was heard in Yorkton. The newlyweds drove to the hearing. Letters that Iser had written to Esther were read in the court. Boring as

Laura Shatsky, the woman who won his heart, Pelly, 1923

Mother said they were, the judge found for the plaintiff. Iser was ordered to pay court costs and $600 in damages — a veritable fortune. Esther's life, however, went from bad to worse. Love eluded her. So did marriage and a family. When, in the early 1940s, she was on her death bed still a relatively young woman, she asked a friend to call Iser. When my father sat down beside her bed, she cried a little, then told him that she had always regretted suing him for breach of promise, that she had never really wanted to do it, but that her uncle and family had insisted. She forgave him for the grief he had caused her. And, of course, my father forgave her.

When Laura and Iser's first child was due, Iser arranged with Doctor Tran, the physician and surgeon in Kamsack, to come the twenty-five miles to Pelly to perform the delivery. He had calculated the baby's arrival to a Sunday in the middle of May. When Laura awoke that particular morning complaining of a stomach-ache, Iser just smiled and suggested that she accompany him to see a patient who lived on a farm a few miles out of town. It was spring and the roads were passable, if a little bumpy. Afterwards, they decided to look for crocuses and birds' nests in the Assiniboine Valley. When Laura continued to complain that her stomach wouldn't settle down, they drove home, arriving at about four o'clock. The tummy-ache persisted, so Iser phoned Doctor Tran.

Marcelyn, however, arrived a good hour before Doctor Tran did, which pleased my father immensely.

A few weeks after Marcelyn's birth, Dr. Tran asked Iser if he would drive down from time to time to assist with surgery at the Kamsack General Hospital. This was an opportunity not to be missed, even though it could take as much as seven hours to get there and a whole day if one got stuck in the mud. But Iser wanted to operate in conditions that were more than makeshift. He was, after all, a surgeon as well as a physician. It was this experience that soon

Iser, Marcie and Laura Steiman, Winnipeg, 1929

convinced him that he needed hospital facilities if he were to give his patients the best of care.

Iser and Laura were happy in their new house in Pelly and loathe to uproot themselves. Nevertheless, in the fall of 1928, they packed their bags and moved to Kamsack, the place of my birth, to begin developing a new practice. Iser made arrangements to do his surgery at the Kamsack General which, although owned by Dr. Tran, was administered by the formidable, two-hundred-and-fifty-pound matron, Mrs. Russell.

Twenty-four-years-older than my father, Tran was good-looking, blond and blue-eyed, and quite the ladies' man according to some accounts. He had been born in Barrie, Ontario in 1874. After completing his MD in 1912, he moved to Kamsack, where he became a powerful figure. In 1915 he was elected mayor, an office he would hold again from 1922 through 1926. In 1925, he was elected a Progressive Party MLA and sat in the Saskatchewan Legislature until 1929. To all intents and purposes, he ran the town of Kamsack.

Among Iser's most interesting cases during his first year in Kamsack was that of Agnes McKie. Dr. Tran had decided to commit her to the mental hospital in Brandon, Manitoba and had asked Dr. Wallace to co-sign her committal papers. This young woman had been a popular and highly-thought-of Salvation Army worker in Winnipeg until she had suddenly taken ill. Because she thereafter refused either to eat or to speak, her superiors, in desperation, sent her home to Kamsack, where her condition continued to deteriorate.

Iser and Laura Steiman, Pelly, 1928

Since then, she had lain in her childhood bed, apparently waiting to die. Apart from drinking a little water, the only thing she would do was get up to wash herself each day.

If Agnes was going to be removed to a facility where her life might be forcibly saved, it would have to be done quickly, but Dr. Wallace was worried about co-signing her committal papers and asked Iser to examine her before he did so. Iser, intrigued, agreed.

Agnes's mother, a tall, gaunt, unsmiling woman, was feeding her brood of children when Iser arrived at the McKie farm. She looked up at him and asked, "Are you the Jew doctor?"

Taken aback, but only for a moment, he replied, "Yes, I'm the Jew doctor. I've come to examine your daughter — if you'll allow me."

She led him through the sparsely furnished house to a small, spotlessly clean bedroom. A young woman was lying in a narrow bed placed in the middle of the room as if it were her coffin.

Iser pulled up a wooden chair and sat down. "Miss McKie," he said, "I was asked by Dr. Wallace to come and see you. Now, is there anything you can tell me about yourself? I'd like to help you."

No answer.

He stayed there a half-hour, observing her, asking her about everything he could think of, but she wouldn't say a thing. Before he left, he talked to her mother. "I can see that she doesn't want to talk to me right now, but I'd like to come back to see her tomorrow."

"I kinna pay you, doctor," Mrs. McKie said apologetically.

"Don't worry about it, Mrs. McKie."

For several weeks, Iser drove out to the McKie farm after lunch. Each time he would ask Agnes, "What started this?"

No answer.

"I understand you were doing good work in the Salvation Army?"

No answer.

"Why should a perfectly healthy girl like you suddenly want to die? Because you surely will if you keep this up."

No answer.

"What happened? You are clean and honest. You had a lot of friends. Was your captain too tough on you? Didn't you have a nice place to live?"

No answer.

One day he told her that Dr. Tran and Dr. Wallace were going to co-sign committal papers to send her to a mental institution if he agreed with their diagnosis. "Do you know what they'll do to you there?"

No answer.

"They'll shove a tube down your throat and force-feed you. They'll give you electric shock treatment. I know, because I interned at that place. You'll wake up one day, look in a mirror and your hair will be filthy, your face bloated and you won't even recognize yourself. You want that?"

No answer.

"Think about it. I'll be back tomorrow."

When Iser returned the next day, Agnes was just as unresponsive as ever. He was at his wits' end. He went to the window and stared out. He was getting nowhere with this patient. She was such a puzzle. A beautiful young woman . . . . Suddenly the answer struck him.

He took a plunge in the dark: "By the way, what happened to your boyfriend?"

Agnes started to cry.

Between sobs, her story began to emerge, as she spoke her first words in weeks. It seems she had been engaged to a young man who was a travelling salesman. They had quarrelled after he made a suggestion that did not fit with her strict Salvation Army principles. An hour or two later, he was killed in an automobile accident on the road to Portage la Prairie.

"Well," Iser said gently, "you didn't kill him, Agnes. You're a very beautiful woman and he must have loved you very much. But you did not cause his death. After all, he could have been killed a week earlier at that same place. I'm sure he would have come back to you if he had lived. There's no reason for you to feel guilty."

As Agnes started to regain her strength, Iser worried about what he could do to get her away from the socially sterile atmosphere of her parents' farm. Knowing that she was unlikely to refuse any reasonable request he might make of her, he asked a favour. "You know, I have a little baby and Mrs. Steiman is so busy helping me with my practice that she doesn't get much chance to take the baby out in her carriage. Would you have time to do this once in a while?" Of course, Agnes agreed.

Iser also knew that Laura would not only give her a good meal when she brought Marcelyn back, but that their conversation would cover a range of topics never touched on in the McKie household.

Such was Agnes's recovery that, within the year, Iser offered her a full-time job in his office in the Harvey Block. She was not a nurse but she was bright and spotlessly clean. Besides, she was a local girl who knew all his patients (as well as being a walking testimonial to his skill as a physician).

Sometime after this, Dr. Wallace told Iser, "I see you have the McKie girl working for you. You know, I could really kick myself when I think about how close I came to signing those papers of Tran's to send her to the asylum. She would never have recovered from that!"

I never heard my father speak ill of any doctor, but after a couple of years in Kamsack, he became uneasy about rumours associated with the Kamsack General. It would appear that everyone, except my father, had come to the conclusion that Mrs. Russell and Dr. Tran were performing illegal abortions. One day in 1932, he decided to broach the question to Mrs. Russell.

"I'm surprised," he began in his best diplomatic manner, "that there are so many young females with appendectomies and miscarriages in here." Mrs. Russell gave him a hard stare. Iser, who in his life never favoured the direct approach in a potentially awkward situation if an oblique one could be found, continued, "The other day, someone suggested that this may be due in some way to the quality of the water in Saskatchewan. What do you think?"

Mrs. Russell took this as a direct criticism of the way she ran the hospital. Her face turned red. Her enormous body seemed to swell to twice its size. Hissing like a puff adder, she picked up the thing nearest to hand, which happened to be a wicker basket filled with artificial flowers but weighted with a brick, and flung it at Father. It struck him on the head. His forehead cut, a little stunned, but not badly hurt, Iser beat a hasty retreat as Mrs. Russell moved to attack him with a coat rack. Later that day, Iser complained to Dr. Tran, who refused to discuss the matter. Iser's friends advised him to lay a charge, on principle. He then went to the Kamsack chief of police, who told him that it was his right to lay a charge if he felt the situation warranted this "extreme response." Iser did.

Mrs. Russell was duly brought before the local justice of the peace where, after what Iser later remembered as a farcical hearing, she was found guilty of common assault and fined one dollar.

Late one evening, a week or so later, a ten-year-old boy was brought into Iser's office with acute appendicitis. An immediate operation was necessary. He carried the boy over to the hospital, where he was confronted by Mrs. Russell, standing four-square barring the door.

"Dr. Tran has cancelled your privileges here."

"My God, woman, this boy is about to die!"

"Take him to Canora."

"At night, over these roads? Are you crazy?"

Mrs. Russell just glared at him.

Iser was furious. "If this boy dies, I'll drag you and Tran through every court in the land." Turning to the boy's parents, he said, "Come on, I'll get Dr. Wallace to give the anaesthetic and we'll operate in my office." (Dr. Wallace was employed by the Department of Indian Affairs to attend to the needs of the two reservations nearby.)

The boy survived, but Iser finally had to face the fact that he could no longer use the Kamsack General Hospital. And, without the use of a hospital, he and Laura might as well have stayed in Pelly. They talked the situation over. In the circumstance, Iser's practice was bound to decline. They had financial responsibility not only for themselves and their baby but, to some considerable degree, for Iser's parents and his seven-year-old brother, Boris. It was with considerable regret that they decided they would have to move.

They began their search by going to the Lakehead (Thunder Bay), where two of Iser's medical school chums had set up practice: Bechford in Port Arthur and Diamond in Fort William (where Great-aunt Rose and Great-uncle Jake lived). Both doctors thought they could use a multilingual partner and Iser was greatly tempted to accept one or other of their offers. On the train back to Kamsack, however, he could not sleep. As opposed to Benito, where he had first set up practice, he liked Kamsack. Laura had made him a comfortable home there and he had a good practice. And what was more, he did not want to admit defeat. There had to be another way. As he told Laura, "If I leave now, I'll be in the category of a beaten dog. We're going to stay and carry on."

As he considered his options, he realized he was not alone. A number of doctors from the surrounding district had stopped using the Kamsack General, travelling the thirty-five miles to Canora instead. Further, Mrs. Russell's villainous behaviour in turning away the critically ill little boy had sparked the outrage of many of the townsfolk, who had felt for a long time that a new hospital was needed. In fact, by standing up to Mrs. Russell and Dr. Tran, Iser had become somewhat of a hero.

In February of 1931 a new hospital board was formed to consider setting up a Kamsack union hospital. This board was unique in that its members represented a variety of religious denominations. The town council voted a $500 grant on condition that the rural municipalities it would serve would also contribute $500. As luck would have it, a large, well-built brick house at the corner of Second Street and Fifth Avenue was about to become vacant. Three storeys high, with a veranda on three sides and surrounded by large trees, it had become the property of the town when the old couple who owned it had been unable to pay the taxes. When approached, the newly elected Kamsack town council not only offered it to Iser at a very reasonable price but promised a moratorium on taxes for as long as it remained a hospital. Thus, in November 1932, did Kamsack's King Edward Hospital come into being.

Iser moved everything from his office into the new hospital. He transferred his x-ray and fluoroscope to a room in the basement which he designated the laboratory. He bought new second-hand equipment for the operating room from Claude Hyman, with whom his credit was always good. The town council gave Iser the ten beds, blankets and other equipment they had purchased during the influenza epidemic of 1919.

On the main floor he set up an operating room and a separate delivery room. Two large adjoining rooms were used for maternity and surgical cases. Laura made curtains and set up the nursery. Four bedrooms upstairs became wards. The attic served as staff quarters. The laundry, kitchen and staff dining room were in the basement. Eventually the large empty lot on the south side of the hospital was turned into a vegetable garden, the harvests from which were used in the hospital kitchen. No one was ever denied treatment in this hospital. Often, cash-strapped farmers paid their bills in chickens and eggs.

Miss Lucille Watson was recruited as the King Edward Hospital's matron. In the beginning, she was the entire nursing staff. A little later, Iser purchased another house and had it moved onto a foundation next to the hospital. This became the nurses' residence. As things turned out, graduates of the Toronto and Winnipeg hospitals were in plentiful supply during the Great Depression and eager to come to work in Kamsack for $25 a month.

King Edward Hospital, Cherie Steiman in foreground, Kamsack, 1936

One of Iser's classmates, the Chaplinesque Dr. Shubin, once came to visit from Winnipeg. After touring the hospital's spotless wards and inspecting everything, he sighed, "You are a king, Iser. You don't know what I have to do to make a living! You never have trouble getting a bed for your patients and they can never take advantage of you as they do in the city. I get called up in the middle of the night: 'Dr. Shubin, my husband is dying! Come quickly!' I get up, wash, dress quickly, hop into the car and rush to the patient's house, only to find two of my colleagues already on the doorstep. All of us have been told to come quickly. The first doctor gets to treat the patient and if he's lucky he will get a handshake in which he'll discover a dollar or two for his troubles. We consider two dollars a very good fee! How long can one carry on a practice like that?"

Ten miles west of Kamsack on the way to Canora was the little settlement of Veregin, named after the leader of the Doukhobors, Peter Vasilevich Verigin (but misprinted on the official map). Dr. George Black, also a graduate of the University of Manitoba Medical School, was practicing there when Iser arrived in Kamsack. After Father set up the King Edward Hospital in 1932, Dr. Black often brought his patients in for surgery. But he had a difficult time in Veregin since he spoke no Russian. Eventually he grew weary of the demands of his patients and moved to Winnipeg to set up practice.

One day in early January, the railway clerk at the Veregin Station put through a call for Dr. Steiman. A fight had broken out during a Doukhobor wedding celebration and some people had been injured. "Need the Doc, fast," he said. Iser jumped into his snowmobile-ambulance and took off. (Iser and John Doochenko, the mechanic at Kamsack's Star Garage, had designed

Iser and Cherie Steiman and John Doochenko with the "Silver Streak" Snowmobile Ambulance, Kamsack, 1938

and built the first snowmobile to be used as an ambulance on the Prairies. They called it the "Silver Streak.")

When Iser entered the large verandahed house at Veregin, people crowded around as he examined a man lying on the floor with his brains spilling out. Iser declared him dead and scooped up a bit of the man's brains as evidence.

"What's been going on here?" Iser asked in Russian.

Nobody answered.

Finally someone whispered, "Our leader exercised his right."

His "right" was to bed the sixteen-year-old bride first, while her father, her new husband and the rest of the wedding party waited outside the door, listening. The story, so far as Iser was able to determine, was that the bride's father, emboldened by liquor and egged on by the groom, had attempted to put a stop to it by beating on the door. But before he could break it down, he was set upon by "the faithful" and killed. A donnybrook ensued.

Iser, after he had treated the injured, told the assembled, "I'll have to notify the police. Charges will have to be laid."

To which the Doukhobor leader replied, "I do not recognize their authority. I am in charge here."

Back at the hospital, after informing the provincial police (there never was a prosecution), Iser was putting a bottle on his specimen shelf when Laura entered. "Whatever is that?" she asked.

He held up the bottle to the light. "Kazakoff's brains," he replied as he set it on the shelf next to McLaren's appendix.

Iser's facility with languages was to come in handy in more ways than one. As a doctor in a small Canadian prairie town in the 1920s and 1930s who could speak Russian, Ukrainian and German, Iser knew almost everyone and a lot more about them than just the state of their bowels. He had become friendly with a mysterious man of whom my mother never approved. Victor Kafte, a dark, lean, strong, good-looking man, sensual like a gypsy, was a jack-of-all-trades who worked about Iser and Laura's boathouse at Madge Lake. Rumour had it that he came from an aristocratic family. Mother had her doubts: "A Count of no account is more likely," she observed. Years later, I heard he had been under surveillance by the RCMP; that he was an informer who reported to the RCMP; that he was a Communist; that he was a double agent. Who knows? The Kamsack of my memory, that sleepy dusty little town, may in fact have been a hotbed of radical unionism and communism, riddled and positively writhing with political revolutionaries, even nudists. I do know that the self-appointed leader of the Kamsack Communist cell was the barber,

Dominion Day Parade, Kamsack, 1938

an illiterate Russian who had, unfortunately, lost most of his nose so that his voice was most peculiar (to say nothing of his face).

The town watchmaker, an elderly man who had fled Russia before the revolution, was also a Communist party member. He spoke excellent Russian and was well-read in Russian literature. He lived alone and had a good collection of Russian books. He was one patient with whom my father enjoyed having long discussions. It was in late August of 1939, just after the signing of the German-Soviet Non-Aggression Pact, that the watchmaker came to ask Iser a favour. He had been warned, possibly by Victor Kafte, to expect a visit from the RCMP. He felt sure that because of his activities in Russia, the Mounties would confiscate his books and charge him with some crime, since his books were written by "revolutionaries" like Tolstoy. My father tried to assure him that no harm would come to him, but the watchmaker was adamant, since that was how the Tsarist secret police had operated in Russia when he was young. So my father agreed to take the box of books for safekeeping and hide it in the attic of our house, the first place any self-respecting policeman would search. The old watchmaker then disappeared.

A few days later, I overheard my mother talking to Katie, our hired girl, as they worked in the kitchen. Katie was cleaning silver and Mother was making a big pot of bean and barley soup. "The RCMP are coming today," she laughed.

The RCMP are coming. The Royal Canadian Mounted Police. I put down my dolls and poked my head out from around the basement door. Mother was stirring the soup, Katie polishing the forks. I had been playing on the steps. I looked down into the dark basement. A troop of Red Coats galloped into my mind, reining in their magnificent steeds at the gate of our house in a cloud of dust. The tallest and straightest (a dead ringer for Nelson Eddy) dismounted, strode up to the front door and pounded on it. "I've come for the *vildeh hyah*," he announced. Fear bordering on terror gripped me. I was finally caught. But for what this time? I hadn't killed any cats, stolen any more babies, or burned down any houses for at least two weeks. Then I knew. I had never returned the empty chocolate milk bottle as I had promised Mr. Avrin, the storekeeper.

Somehow I managed to extricate myself from this childhood vision of hell to climb back up into the kitchen.

"Mommy," I asked innocently, "why are the RCMP coming here?"

"Oh," she smiled, "Daddy told me they wanted to look at the books in the library."

"Is that all?" I gave an enormous sigh of relief. Obviously, my latest crime had passed undetected.

Just off our living room was my father's library. Shelves and shelves of books lined the walls. There were books of all kinds in English, German, French, Russian, Hebrew, Latin and Yiddish. Father received catalogues from booksellers all over the world and spent hours in used bookstores wherever he went. This was one of the reasons he so loved New York, where he often went during the 1930s to take medical refresher courses, where once for six weeks he'd worked in one of the city's free clinics (where he said he learned more medicine than he had in the previous five years in Kamsack). Cartons of books would follow his suitcases off the train whenever he returned. Sometimes I would take one of his medical books down from the shelf and hide under the grand piano to peer in appalled wonderment at the photographs of naked bodies, or parts thereof, covered with boils or other disgusting conditions. Now I wondered why the RCMP wanted to look as well. Needless to say, no troop of Mounties arrived to tear apart our house or search father's library book by book. No one came to lift the floor boards of the attic to uncover the stash of dangerous literature hidden there. And I'm really sorry they didn't. It would have been a great adventure for my father, but the old watchmaker simply returned after a month or so, collected his books and resumed his watchmaking.

As the King Edward Hospital flourished, the Kamsack General deteriorated. It simply couldn't compete. Dr. Tran finally decided to move away to set up practice on the West Coast. This obviously did not suit him because he returned not long afterwards, suffered a stroke while attending a patient and was admitted to the Kamsack General where he died in 1934 at the age of sixty. That hospital eventually closed in 1937.

The records for 1938 show that the King Edward Hospital had a most successful year. Three sets of twins were brought into the world and seven hundred and fifty-one patients treated. By the time the Second World War broke out in September 1939, the King Edward Hospital was operating smoothly with twenty-five beds, serving the rural municipalities of Calder, Sliding Hills, Coté, Togo and Veregin. It had a good staff, which usually included one or two young medical graduates who would spend a year or two at the hospital before going off to establish their own practices. Indeed, the hospital was so busy that Iser had to hire Mr. Harvey, a former mayor of Kamsack, as a business manager to help administer its affairs.

F L Y I N G   H I G H

It would have been easy for Iser to sit out the war enjoying the peace and plenty that his years of hard work had earned him, had he been so inclined. He was forty-one, married and the father of two children — not a prime candidate for military service. The very idea of staying at home when others were going off to battle the evil forces of Nazism, however, was repugnant to him. He wrote to the Canadian Army about joining the medical corps. When he did not receive a reply, he caught the train for Regina in early January, 1940 to volunteer in person.

At the recruiting depot, he found himself in line with his friend Gary Isman, who had been his roommate in medical school. Despite their ages, the Army welcomed them, assigning them the rank of First Lieutenant Royal Canadian Army Medical Corps. They were then told to go back to their respective practices and sit tight until they were called up for active service. This was not good enough for Iser. He immediately left for Winnipeg, where he transferred to the Royal Canadian Air Force (RCAF), a Service with an immediate need for doctors.

Iser's first duties were at the RCAF recruiting centre in Winnipeg, giving physical examinations to the hundreds of young men who were flocking into town to enlist as pilots and air gunners. After several months of this, he was transferred to the #7 Bombing and Gunnery School, near Dauphin, Manitoba. The school was nothing more than a couple of runways and a few hastily-thrown-up barracks on what had been some farmer's wheat field. As medical officer, he was responsible for keeping the Canadian and British bomber and ground crews fit. To the homesick young pilots, the steadying hand of a good and sympathetic physician meant everything. They knew that in Iser they could always find a friendly father confessor to whom they could tell their troubles. And, because of his wide experience as a rural family physician, he soon became the "anchor man," the touchstone for many a young Canadian medical man whose education had been telescoped to give the RCAF the number of physicians it required.

One of Iser's jobs at the Bombing and Gunnery School was to go out with the Rescue Team to pick up the pieces after the occasional mid-air collision. It was shortly after one of these accidents that a member of his enlisted medical staff knocked on his office door to announce that a civilian female wished to see him.

"What does she want?"

"She won't say. She just wants to see you."

A middle-aged woman came in, holding a picture of her son, one of the young men who had been killed a couple of weeks before. She asked Iser if he had seen him after he died.

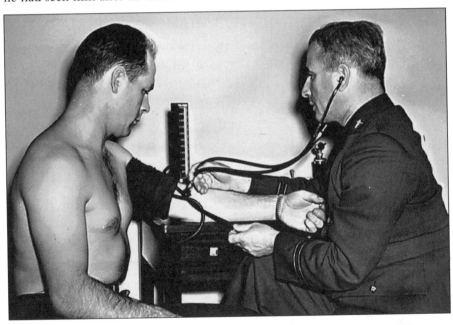

Flight Lieutenant Iser Steiman, 1943

"Yes," he told her.

"How did he look?"

"Just the same as his picture," he lied.

Years later, remembering this incident, my father broke down: "All those splendid young men that I passed as fit to fly, only to see them killed."

Whenever Iser had a few days' leave, he took the train to Kamsack to visit Mother, Marcie and me, and to check on the hospital. (Sometime later, he decided to sell a share of the hospital to Dr. Alvin Cohen, who ran it along with Mr. Harvey for the duration of the war.)

In the fall of 1942, Iser and Laura spent his two-week furlough in New York visiting friends, seeing shows and, respectively, shopping and haunting second-hand bookstores. One afternoon, Iser wandered into a Russian-language Workers' Book Store on East 13th Street. After looking over the Soviet propaganda that filled the shop, on impulse he asked the clerk if it would be possible for him to order certain Russian books on anatomy, surgery, physiology, aviation medicine and military field surgery. The clerk wrote all this down, took Iser's Manitoba address and promised to find out. Iser, however, left the shop expecting never to hear another word about it.

Iser's real interest at the time was aviation medicine (the psychological, physiological and pathological effects of flying), an enthusiasm sparked by the month-long course he had just finished in Toronto. There were no English-language texts on the subject because, after the First World War, interest in aviation was confined almost entirely to the civilian sphere. Consequently, there had been no government research in any of the Allied nations into pilot fatigue, body stress or the kinds of injuries sustained in plane crashes and parachute jumping. It occurred to Iser that the Soviets, who were now joined in the war against Hitler's Germany, might be an untapped source of information on aviation medicine. When he brought this up in class, one of his lecturers, Air Commodore J. W. Tice, replied, "Oh, those Russians! They're just a bunch of conscripts. They don't have a damn thing!"

But it seemed to Iser that Tice might be wrong. The Soviets and the Germans had been cooperating on military matters, and on aviation in particular, since the early 1920s. It seemed to him that as the Germans were the only ones who had prepared for this war, it was possible that the Russians might have had the chance to borrow from them in this vital area of medicine.

A few weeks after his return from New York to his post, which was now

#2 Bombing & Gunnery near Portage la Prairie, he received a letter from New York, advising him that the Workers' Book Store was holding five books on military medicine for him, including The Fundamentals of Aviation Medicine (Moscow, 1939, 379 pages). If he would kindly send a money order for ten dollars, these would be forwarded to him directly.

As soon as Iser realized that his suspicions had been confirmed and that all the basic research on high altitude physiology and motion sickness was indeed in the Russian text, he alerted his friend, Wing Commander J.K.W. Ferguson, at the School of Aviation Medicine in Toronto (who had been seconded into the RCAF from the Chair of Pharmacology at the University of Toronto). Ferguson, in turn, arranged to have Iser and his startling find introduced to the leading American neurophysiologist, Professor John F. Fulton at Yale University. Fulton, a Harvard pupil of Harvey Cushing (the great American neurosurgeon) and an Oxford PhD from the laboratory of Sir Charles Sherrington (1932 Nobel Prize in Physiology), was at the very cross-roads of the physiological war effort. As Iser later recalled, a visit to the High Altitude Research Group at New Haven might have led one to believe that the entire Allied cause was directed from that city. It was in this rarefied atmosphere that Iser would do the major work on his English translation of all his Russian books. His days in the Bombing and Gunnery schools were now behind him.

When he had finished the translation of The Fundamentals of Aviation Medicine, he was somewhat confused and disappointed by Ottawa's apparent lack of interest. It was only when the National Research Council in Washington, DC, impressed by the manuscript, offered to publish it immediately that Ottawa decided it was "hot." Squadron Leader Edgar Black of the Banting and Best Institute, who had worked mainly on the respiratory effects of flying and had much to do with the invention of the pressure mask worn by air crew, was now placed in charge of the fine editing and actual publication of the book. And that is how The Fundamentals of Aviation Medicine in its English translation came into being in July 1943.

Once published, of course, the book became "classified" material, restricted to certain Allied medical officers only. Even Edgar Black was not allowed a copy. Instead, he stole the one intended for Iser and suggested Iser write to Air Commodore Tice for another, which he did. Tice complied, but apparently was not amused. His covering letter stated: "It is my duty to remind you that this publication is to be treated as a confidential document."

Iser, whose mind-set could hardly be described as military, could never understand why a volume which he had purchased over the counter of a Communist bookstore in New York was given classified status, especially when its contents in all likelihood had been extracted from German sources in the first place (something he confirmed when he visited Russia in 1956 and met some of the scientists at the Pavlov Institute who were supposed to have written the book).

In the meantime, John Fulton, anxious to have Iser formally seconded to his research unit at Yale, wrote to the RCAF requesting his services for the duration of the war. Ottawa flatly refused. Professor Fulton, however, was not to be denied. He simply wired British Air Marshall Sir Harold E. Whittington in London and explained what he wanted. Whittington put on the pressure and Iser received his posting to the hush-hush aeromedical research unit located in the basement of the medical school at Yale, where he continued with his translations of Russian military medical texts and conducted his own research into frostbite.

Although my father could not have been more pleased with the way in which things had worked out, nor with the high regard in which he was held by Dr. Fulton and his associates, he always felt that Fulton went well beyond the call of duty to make him feel at home. Dr. and Mrs. Fulton had provided him a suite of rooms in their mansion. But for some strange reason, his towels, serviettes, even his soap were embossed with Russian emblems. And Fulton apologized profusely for not being able to obtain venison for him, as if Iser had just arrived from the steppes of Russia.

When he was not translating or conducting experiments, Iser immersed himself in the Yale medical library, which held the priceless collections of Cushing, Fulton and Edwin Klebs (German-American pathologist, 1834-1913, who pioneered in the study of infectious diseases). His passion, however, became Elie von Cyon, the teacher of Ivan Petrovich Pavlov at the University of St. Petersburg. I am certain that Iser collected everything that von Cyon ever wrote, or that was ever written about him. And although his personal library bulged with books on every branch of medical history, von Cyon was accorded first place in all discussions and book acquisitions. (His von Cyon collection now resides in the Woodward Biomedical Library at the University of British Columbia.)

As to what happened to the rest of us while my father was off doing his

Laura, Marcie and Cherie Steiman, Winnipeg, 1942

bit for King, country and the advancement of medical science, Mother soon decided that she was "not going to spend the duration stuck in that hole of a town". Nor was she about to move us all in with her parents in Pelly. She was not that kind of a woman. She arranged for her brother Lawrence, who was now running the Kamsack Produce, to move into our house with his wife just for the duration and in July of 1940, she drove the two hundred and fifty miles of rough washboard gravel roads to Winnipeg to find us a decent place to live, which in her mind meant anywhere but North Winnipeg's New Jerusalem.

To the scandal of assorted Steimans, Shatskys and Finns, she found us a one-bedroom apartment in a red brick building called the River Heights Apartments at 378 Academy Road, far away from all our meddling kin. Wartime housing was at a premium and in order to achieve this triumph of personal independence, she not only had to "smear" (bribe) the owner, but agree to pay the exorbitant rent of $53.50 a month. "It's only until Iser has finished his war," she rationalized, "which is not going to be all that long, so maybe we can afford it." She then drove back to Kamsack, packed up the car, leaving just enough room for Marcie and me, and headed fearlessly for the big city. As things turned out, we spent five years in Winnipeg.

Becoming accustomed to life in a small apartment took some doing. In Kamsack, we had lived in a large, four-bedroom house. Now Mother, Marcie and I shared a single bedroom and an upright piano was pushed into the corner of our breakfast nook. But even I understood that it was wartime and we all had to make a special effort. So we did. Mother worked for the Red Cross and Marcie and I collected every bit of string we could find, smoothed out the silver paper from the packs of Export cigarettes Mother smoked, and saved newspapers. And we all knitted scarves and socks and balaclavas for our soldiers overseas. It was all very exciting. But my principal fascination was our neighbours. In my young life, I had never lived so close to so many people and I followed their comings and goings assiduously.

Our apartment was a corner suite, number 14, on the third floor. Next door lived the diminutive Mrs. Beaton and her daughters, Marilyn (about twelve) and Jane (about twenty-one, whose young husband had been just sent overseas) and Jane's two-year-old son, Roger. Marilyn, a big pudding of a girl, looked like her father, Colonel Beaton, who would appear whenever he had leave, which was seldom. Jane, however, was totally different in appearance from either of her parents. Not particularly pretty, but tall and slender with long, shapely legs and beautiful hands with the longest and most perfectly manicured nails that I had ever seen. Every morning she left the apartment dressed to the nines. When we discovered she was a professional model, we were amazed.

"A model," Mother gasped. "How can she be a model with that face?" But it was true. She appeared regularly in magazines and the newspapers and catalogues — that is, her legs appeared in ads for stockings, her hands in ads for gloves and jewellery, and her body in bathing suits and fine apparel, her face always turned discreetly to the left, or right, or behind a veil or hidden by a hat.

One day in 1943, a young boy in a CNR Telegraph messenger's uniform came to the apartment block. I watched as he mounted the three flights of stairs and knocked on the Beatons' door. In those days, the very sight of a telegraph messenger struck fear into the hearts of everyone who saw him approaching their door. Who was wounded, missing, killed? As it turned out, Jane's young husband had been killed in action. I did not venture past their door for days, but took a long detour down one flight and through another hallway, afraid to disturb a mourning I did not understand. When Jane finally returned to work, the next advertisement featured her lying on studio sand modelling the latest swimsuit, a large sombrero covering her entire head. So no one but us ever got to see the sadness in her eyes.

Mrs. Hornby lived in apartment number 17. Marilyn and I always held our noses and giggled whenever we passed her door. Short and fat, with frizzy blue hair, Mrs. Hornby had a weak bladder. I often passed her on the staircase wiping up, rather ashamedly, the little puddles she had dropped. The red runner in front of her door took the worst of it as she struggled with her key, however, which accounted for the stench that rose to greet each passer-by.

Mrs. Stapleton in number 19 was always losing her diamond ring or other valuables, or so she claimed. Certainly, she spent a lot of time with Mr. Jenkins, the janitor, going through the garbage in the incinerator room down in the basement, which may not have been as unpleasant as it appeared to me at the time. It was warm and dark down there. And Jenkins was, after all, a man, of which gender there was a considerable shortage at the time.

For myself, I was convinced Mr. Jenkins was a spy. I was one Canadian patriot who took her war business seriously. I had studied all the posters and had taken their lessons to heart. "THE WALLS HAVE EARS." "LOOSE LIPS SINK SHIPS." We had to do our bit. Strange noises occasionally came from Mr. Jenkins' apartment opposite the furnace room in the basement. Clickings and tappings. Irregular tappings. And always just after supper. I convinced Marilyn next door that something sinister was going on. We pressed our ears to his door. Morse code, of course. For weeks we watched him cleaning the halls, burning the trash. We followed him everywhere. One night, hoping to catch him red-handed sending messages to the Huns, I ran upstairs, leaving Marilyn posted at his door and insisted my sister Marcie come down to listen as well. "Oh, don't be so stupid," she said. "Don't you know he's teaching himself to type? He doesn't want to be a janitor all his life." Win some, lose some: nine is not an easy age for a girl.

Neither is ten. Down on the main floor lived another manless family: Mrs. McKegg and her two daughters. She was a short, round-faced, cheery woman with ruddy cheeks and blue eyes, a turned-up nose and a bright smile. I spent a lot of time with the younger daughter, but especially liked the mother. Returning to our apartment in early September 1943, after having spent the two-month summer holiday in Saskatchewan with my grandparents, I was horrified to find the McKeggs were no longer living in their apartment. A new name, a strange name, appeared on their mailbox in the entrance hall. When I asked my mother where they were, she told me that Mrs. McKegg had died and that the two girls had been sent to live with an aunt in another part of Winnipeg. How or when she had died, I was never told, but I was overcome with sadness . . . and fear. How could a woman so pink and healthy and cheerful only two months before, die and disappear? And if it could happen to Mrs. McKegg, might it not happen to my mother? I need not have worried — Mother would live for another forty-three years — but worry I did.

Wives of those of my father's colleagues who had not "joined up" (and were "staying at home making a fortune") would phone Mother with invitations for Friday night dinners or Saturday night parties but when she informed them that Father was not home on leave, they would terminate the conversation with a, "Well, perhaps next time." Apparently, they could not cope with odd numbers. So most Friday and Saturday nights, Mother worked at the Armed Services canteen. She and Ruthie Singer, a teenager who lived in the apartment below us with her stern, widowed mother, would take the streetcar down to Portage and Main streets, not far from Eaton's Department Store, where the canteen was located. Ruthie worked as a coat-check girl, heaving the heavy coarse khaki great-coats, damp with snow, onto hangers. Mother worked as short-order cook, frying bacon and eggs, hamburgers and onions and making pies — sometimes as many as forty at a time. Later on the way home, Ruthie, sitting next to my mother, would lean over and sniff her coat and say, "You smell of bacon." My mother would return the compliment, "And you smell of wet wool." And they would laugh and laugh until the streetcar stopped at Ash and Academy Road.

Often a friend of Mother's would invite us to her house for dinner. Sarah Nitikman lived down the street from us in a big house with her three children, two boys and a girl. She was widowed and related in some way to someone in Kamsack. She and my mother were both manless and all of us children fatherless. We looked forward to dinners at her house. Sarah was fat, had reddish hair, wore glasses and seemed to be a rather cheerful person, considering all her problems. Bert, the younger boy, looked like her: he had flaming hair and freckles and was full of the devil. Her oldest, Allan, was tall, gangling, freckled and quiet. Her daughter, Lee, was beautiful. She had brown hair and a good figure. She was the first person I'd ever met who had had a nose job. But she also suffered from a terrible case of acne, something with which my sister and I were lucky not to have been afflicted. There were endless discussions which went on for months as to what could be done about it. All kinds of concoctions and remedies were tried to no avail. Eventually I was told by my sister that Sarah had taken Lee to a doctor, a specialist who said that her acne would disappear when she got married. This struck me as being a very strange and mysterious cure, but I accepted it as being just another phenomenon of childhood that I could not understand but that would perhaps become clear to me when I grew up.

In spite of rationing, we enjoyed many happy and noisy dinners around Sarah's table that could easily accommodate the odd number seven. She used to make a rich crusty corn pudding which became a favourite with our family, especially my father. And so her memory lives.

SARAH'S CORN PUDDING

1 can creamed corn	1 teaspoon salt
1/4 cup cream of wheat	2 eggs beaten well
1 cup milk	2 tablespoons butter
1 teaspoon sugar	

Preheat oven to 400°F. Put butter into casserole and heat in oven until bubbly. Beat eggs and add to combined ingredients. Pour into hot buttered casserole and bake in a 400° oven, as for a soufflé, until crusty and brown.

During our years in Winnipeg, we usually spent the first Passover Seder at Auntie Lily's house on Pritchard Street in the North End, where all the assorted cousins (Lily's three boys, Manny, Julius and Bernard, Auntie Dora's son, Murray) and Marcie and I would squeeze in around the table. Auntie Lily's husband, Saul Morry and Auntie Dora's husband, Mayer Zaslovsky, were the only adult males present.

Uncle Saul conducted the Seder, reclining on a chair, surrounded by pillows. A shiny black *yarmulke* skated precariously on his shining bald head, sending us into fits of laughter. He stuttered slightly, so the prayers and readings from the Haggadah dragged on and on. The youngest boys asked the four questions amid childish titters and adult corrections.

"*Mah nishtanah hala-y'lah hazeh mikol halaylos?*" (Why is this night different from all other nights of the year?) "*Mah nishtanah . . . Mah nishtanah . . . Mah nishtanah . . .*," sung as they have been sung for thousands of years.

Lily and Dora, both under five feet and big-chested, never got to sit down at the table, although places had been set for them. They spent the entire evening in the kitchen serving course after course of Passover specialities they had slaved over for days: *gefilte fish* (fish balls), with sinus-clearing horseradish; carrot *tzimmes* (that needs to be cooked forever to be really great); and, of course, *matzo balls* in golden ponds of chicken soup.

My mother made *matzo balls* the way her mother made them — light as balloons. Auntie Lily, naturally, made them the way her mother had made them — like cannonballs.

As he cut into one, Manny would pipe up: "Mama, does the Department of Defence know about these?" This, of course, set off the rest of the children.

"The Allies' secret weapon!"

"Depth charges: vra-room!!"

"Bombs away!"

"Mama, Uncle Sam needs you!"

All the while Uncle Saul is shouting over the din, "*Ma-Ma-Mammele, mammele* (little mother) . . . *mammele* come and sit down!"

Auntie Lily appears in the kitchen doorway wrapped in a big white apron, throws up her hands and glares at him as if he is crazy. "*Mammele,*" he cajoles, "another *matzo ball* please."

And so the long evening progresses with endless food and endless rituals. The reading of the entire Haggadah recounting of the story of the Jews in Egypt; the washing of hands; the dipping of parsley in water; the explanation of the symbols — the bitter herbs, the hard life; saltwater, tears; the dramatic recitation of the murrain — plagues of blood, wild beasts, hail, frogs, locusts, vermin, boils, darkness, culminating in the smiting of the firstborn, followed by the exciting escape and pursuit, the parting of the waves, the jubilant freedom.

Squirming in our chairs, we are often told to shush. Falling asleep, we wake just in time to join the search for the *afhikomen* — the hidden *matzo* — the finder gloating over the prize nickel or dime Uncle Saul hands out.

Some people are missing from our Passover table. My uncles Boris and Harold are in England with the Canadian Army and my father is busy at Yale translating top-secret Russian texts. The door is opened to let Elijah the Prophet in. But for me it is not his spirit that enters. It is theirs.

Captain Harold Shatsky, 1940s

Boris and Iser Steiman, Winnipeg, 1942

In the summer of 1944, I was eleven — well, nearly so — and my sister, Marcie, was sixteen. As usual, we had been packed off to spend the two-month school holiday with our grandparents in Pelly. In early August, Grandpa Sam drove us down to Madge Lake where we were to spend a week with friends, the Lomows, who had a cottage there.

August 9th, a Saturday, dawned warm and full of expectation of good times. There was a continuous stream of young people for tennis, swimming, or strawberry picking along the shaded dirt road that led to the beach. A half-holiday had been declared in Kamsack, the nearest town, and a dance was being held that evening in Johnny's Dance Pavilion at the lake, which meant that a lot more people, young and old, would be heading out to the lake for midsummer fun.

By late morning, however, the air had become unusually oppressive, heavy and humid. At the water pump, Victor Kafte said to me, "Storm coming."

"How do you know?" I asked, looking up into his handsome, tanned and leathery face.

"Been around here a long time," he answered, still pumping the handle, "the way the air feels, the sky looks. Wait, you'll see I'm right."

When I got back to the cottage with my pail of water, I announced, "A storm is coming." But nobody was interested. The girls were jabbering about the plans for the day. And my sister seemed to have a problem she could only discuss with Mrs. Lomow.

"Bill asked me to go swimming, but I can't . . . you know . . . I just can't."

It was suffocatingly hot. Why can't she go swimming? I wondered.

Mrs. Lomow looked at my sister knowingly and said, "Why don't you suggest a game of tennis instead?" My sister agreed and ran out the door, leaving me to wonder why she could play tennis but not swim.

The day wore on, hot, heavy and heavier. The road to the lake was hazardous, so washboardy, so fraught with potholes that nobody used it if there was a cloud in the sky, or the remotest possibility of rain. All afternoon, cars and pickup trucks rolled in from Kamsack, sending up huge clouds of dust which eventually settled on the bushes and trees lining the road. Later on, a light warm wind started to blow and the sky became ominously dark. By eight o'clock the wind was tossing the branches wildly about.

My friends and I hung around Johnny's Store and Dance Pavilion in the darkening evening, watching the guys and gals arrive; flirting, primping, swigging from bottles they had stashed in cars or flasks pulled out of back pockets.

The band struck up. Music floated over the lake to the delight of all the little ones tucked up on metal cots or makeshift beds in the clapboard cottages that dotted the shoreline. By ten o'clock, the dance was in full swing.

In Kamsack, the streets were deserted. Not even the hotel beer parlour was doing its usual Saturday night business, although some of the regulars were there. At the CNR station, two or three fellows were loitering under the cover of its extended roof. In the Russell Cafe, Lucy Kasakov was wiping off the last of the tables, while her young son Johnny waited for her at the door.

The Elite Theatre, however, was surprisingly full. Percy Goodland, its manager, who had seen that evening's film several times before, was instead watching the sky darken, the wind rise and thunderclouds roll in. An electrical storm on the prairies is awesome to behold, and fearsome. The crops needed rain, but not too much.

A frantic farmer phoned the police to report a whirlwind of black smoke rolling in from the west and a whitish grey funnel moving across the prairie like a wicked genie. In turn, the police phoned the Elite Theatre to warn Goodland that this was no ordinary storm on the horizon and that he should keep his audience in the theatre until it abated. Just as the lights went up, Percy announced from the stage in a loud, calm voice, "There is a storm warning out and I've been advised that it would not be safe for you to go out into the streets at this time. Everyone please remain seated and calm."

Back in the small lobby, he carefully opened the front door a crack. The wind flung it wide against the wall. It took two strong fellows to help him close it. A few minutes later they heard a crash. They did not know then that the front wall of Elite Confectionery, just two doors down the street, had been ripped off and tossed onto a parked car. As Percy was struggling to close the door, he had caught sight of two flying figures. When Lucy Kasakov, on her way home with her son, had been caught in the initial rainstorm, they dashed into the doorway of the Star Garage. She had clung onto the door handle and he to her until the entire door had been ripped away. Suddenly, they found themselves flung into the street, rolling through the mud like rubber balls. When they recovered sufficiently to sit up, they saw in a flash of

The cyclone, Kamsack, August 1944, courtesy Kamsack Historical Society

lightning that the Star Garage had disappeared.

Lorna Leavens and her brother Lesley were sitting in their dining room, drinking with a couple of friends. When the wind began to rise, she locked the screen door and closed the windows. She was in the middle of a sentence when the lights went out and the furniture started sliding about the room. She grabbed at the table as it slid away and called out to her friends, who were screaming. Then, after a tremendous crash, everything was still.

Lorna struggled up from the floor and looked around her, wondering perhaps if she had passed out and been carried up to the bedroom, for she was certainly no longer in the dining room. In the dark, she bumped into the piano, which had always been downstairs in the living room. Confused, she, her brother and their friends stumbled down the stairs and out the front door. Their house was now sitting back to front in a neighbour's yard.

When old man Popham, who was over eighty, heard the thunder and crashing of buildings all about him and looked across the street to see a house collapsing, he flapped his arms and ran about wildly exclaiming, "It's an attack! The Germans have landed!" He promptly hid himself in the root cellar and wouldn't come out for two days.

In two minutes the wind collapsed three hundred houses, ripped the roof off the Pool elevator, blowing it to smithereens, and destroyed the Unitarian church, the Catholic church and the little synagogue. In addition, every outhouse in the town was knocked over or blown away. The cyclone had had no respect for anything.

Rushing off in a north-easterly direction toward Madge Lake where the dance was in full swing, the cyclone capriciously veered off at the last second, leaving the merrymakers to enjoy their midsummer madness a little longer, blissfully unaware of what horror awaited them on their return to Kamsack.

The next day, Marcie got a ride into town, hoping to be of some help at the hospital, which had remained undamaged, as had our home on Third

Main Street the day after the cyclone hit,
August, 1944

Street. I was forced to stay at the lake with other little ones that day and listen to radio accounts and gossip.

For the next week, Kamsack was news. Headlines across Canada and the U.S. screamed "DISASTER." Radio stations carried eyewitness reports. For that moment in time, everyone knew not only that Kamsack existed but where it was on the map of Canada. Every August the Kamsack Times reruns pictures of the disaster and surviving eyewitnesses are trotted out and interviewed: "Yessir, you betcha, it sure put Kamsack on the map!"

With the help of the army, the town was rebuilt. Life went on as usual. Curiously, however, things were never the same for the local Jews after that wind blew our synagogue down. A new one was built but it was as if the cyclone were an omen. Many of the original Jewish settlers felt it was time to move on, my father and mother among them.

When the war was over, the opportunity arose to sell the King Edward Hospital to the socialist government of Tommy Douglas which eventually replaced it in 1950 with the large modern Kamsack Union Hospital. And after living for five years in Winnipeg, there was no way my mother would go back to "that one-horse town," as she had taken to calling Kamsack, especially now that Marcie was nearly ready to go to university. As for my father, he would be leaving Kamsack a better place than he found it. So all of us — Grandpa Sam, Grandma Elizabeth, Shannon, Lawrence and Harold (lately demobbed) and their wives plus the irreplaceable Mary — packed up and headed straight west for that Garden of Eden, Vancouver!

THE LAST OF
OUR MOHICANS

It is August, 1989. My research is complete. My stories are written. On coming to Vancouver, my father had thrown himself into the task of building a "city practice" with the same pioneering spirit that he'd brought to Benito, Pelly and Kamsack. And it was not long before Doukhobors, White Russians, war refugees, and new Canadians found their way to his office door. His long experience in "pioneer" communities had developed in him a "presence" (some would call it a bedside manner) which breathed confidence into the sick and their distraught families. In addition, he had taken on the mostly thankless, occasionally rewarding task of rehabilitating chronic alcoholics, from society matrons in their sprawling Shaughnessy mansions, to fallen workers, professionals and former business magnates in sordid, east-end hotels. The years passed. My sister Marcie and I completed university. She married a dentist, Sydney Smordin who had been born in Dauphin, Manitoba, and they had three children, Elizabeth, Elaine and Lyle. I married a businessman, Julian Smith, affectionately known as Buddy, of the Calgary Shumiatcher-Smith clan, to which we added two more, Connie and Gary. Our lives were full and busy. There are many stories in those years, but they belong to the fourth and fifth generations, to be written later, possibly by Elizabeth Smordin Morantz, a writer in her own right.

Julian and Cherie Smith, Laura, Marcie
Smordin, Iser, Sid Smordin, Vancouver, 1962

Iser died in 1981 and Laura followed in 1986. I am left sorting through almost a century of photographs, passports, official documents, letters, interview transcripts, recipes. So, what to do with them? The family cookbook I'll keep. As to the rest . . . label them and send them off to Winnipeg to lie in folders in green metal filing cabinets entombed within the Jewish Historical Archives, which are themselves entombed within the vaster provincial archives? But something holds me back, a reluctance to let go. All those faces, all those people in our photograph album — all those lives — their loves, squabbles and feuds, their adventures, misadventures and accomplishments have slipped into a forgotten past. As I try to piece them all together, I realize the responsibility is enormous. As John P. Marquand put it: "We can interpret, but we can never know. All that is certain — and this is as sure as fate — is that all these vanished people made things the way they are."

"What about this one?" I ask, as I look at the photograph of a handsome young man, my father's younger brother Mark, who had stayed on in the Soviet Union. Why would he do such a thing? Had he been he a die-hard Communist? And what happened to my cousin Mara, or indeed her children, his grandchildren? I knew a little. I had to find out the rest.

It was through Auntie Lily that we knew what little we did about Uncle Mark. From the time the Solomon Steiman family arrived in Winnipeg in 1924, my father's oldest sister had maintained a correspondence with their brother in Viatka, and later in Gorky. The Soviet Union's entry into the Second World War in 1940 interrupted this. It was not until late 1945 that Lily received word from Mark's daughter Mara telling her that Mark had been killed in action in 1942. So Lily began to correspond with Mara. Then in 1948, Stalin rang down the Iron Curtain. Russia's citizens were forbidden further contact with the West.

Eight years later in 1956, when my father went to Russia with his friend Dr. David Baltzan from Saskatoon, he tried to contact Mara and her family at their last known address. Gorky, however, was a closed city. No foreigners allowed. On his second trip in 1962, when he went with my mother, he tried again. Gorky was still closed to foreigners, although he did manage to speak briefly with Mara by telephone. She, however, was too ill to travel to Moscow to meet them and no further communication resulted.

So here I am, twenty-seven years after anyone's last contact with Mara, trying to find her, or her daughter Margarita. There are no clues as to their whereabouts. Even their surnames are unknown. Auntie Lily is dead, her letters and address book destroyed. No trace in my parents' address books. Auntie Dora has never had the address and neither had Uncle Boris (who has recently retired as a prominent American sociologist and gerontologist). At last, an old envelope postmarked Gorky is found but the address is half-obliterated.

I write a letter in Russian to Mara Steiman despite the fact that I think it improbable in the extreme that she is still alive, and send it to half an address in Gorky. Of course, it's returned. There is nothing more I can do.

Now an extraordinary thing happens. Just three weeks before my husband Buddy and I are to leave for a month in Russia, my cousin Manny Morry (Lily's son) in Winnipeg phones to read me the copy of a circular letter he has just received:

THE LAST OF OUR MOHICANS

2 August, 1989
204 Sprucewood Terrace
Amherst, NY 14221
USA

Dear Ms. Morry:

I have received a letter from my sister in Gorky, USSR,
that your niece, Rita, is looking for her aunt in Canada.

Rita is a former wife of my nephew, Shmuel Konkolsky.

If you are indeed related to Rita, please get in touch
with me either by mail or phone.

Respectfully,
George M. Alter
phone 716 634-6843

Is this mental telepathy? While I am looking for her, my cousin Margarita is looking for me. I immediately put in a call to Mr. Alter, who explains that his son had gone to the public library to consult the Winnipeg phone book for Lily's address, but not finding her listed, decided to contact all the Morrys in Winnipeg, hoping to reach the right one. He also informs me his niece-by-marriage has two children, Anna and Mark. I know then that she is Uncle Mark's grandchild, and my final missing link.

After coming to power in the Soviet Union in March 1985, Gorbachev began processes that nobody had foreseen. The peoples of the USSR and its satellite states were given back the right to think and speak. Political taboos that had held one-sixth of the world's population in thrall were broken. Eastern Europe was set free. Soviet troops pulled out of Afghanistan. And the East-West confrontation which threatened to pulverize the earth with megatons of nuclear arms began to ease. The Cold War had come to an end. Despite all this, however, in 1989 Gorky remained closed to foreigners.

Margarita (Rita) comes to Moscow to meet us. She and her sixteen-year-old daughter, Anna, catch an early train from Gorky at about 2:30 a.m. and arrive at the hotel in which Buddy and I are staying some six hours later. As I wait in the lobby with Natasha, our interpreter-guide, I wonder aloud how I will be able to recognize her. Natasha tells me not to worry. She will be able to pick her out at once.

"How?" I ask.

"From the way she dresses. She's from the provinces. And she's Jewish."

Before I have time for the implication of her words to sink in, Rita comes through the door. I recognize her immediately. Short and tubby with fair curly hair, a tiny nose and thick-lensed glasses like Grandfather Solomon's — the family resemblance is so strong, she could have been Aunt Lily's daughter. Her daughter Anna, on the other hand, although short and chesty like her mom, has straight brown hair, dark brown eyes and broad Slavic cheekbones.

Once up in our hotel room, which our interpreter-guide refuses to enter, Rita draws from her large carry-all a bottle of *champanski* and a fancy cake for which they have stood in line for hours, in order to celebrate our "historic" meeting. All the while Natasha stands in the doorway, eating cake and translating. However, it soon becomes obvious that Rita and Anna are reluctant to talk about anything important through Natasha, who Rita in turn recognizes as obviously KGB. It is amusing for me, however, to watch Natasha's disdain for these "country bumpkins" change to envy, as I begin to produce the gifts I had brought from "America": Adidas, digital watches, clothes, lipsticks, a state-of-the-art knitting machine for Anna, who has magic hands.

After a good lunch we visit the *beriozhka*, a foreign currency store where Russians are technically prohibited from shopping for it is illegal for them to have foreign currency. However, they are allowed in with us. We stock up on groceries, sugar, coffee, tea, oil, tinned meat and fish, all of which are rationed or almost impossible to buy in Gorky. Rita stands before a case filled with cans of caviar. She wants one to give to Mark's doctor. It's not for eating, it's for bartering. We buy a big tote bag for it all and they depart for Gorky laden down, but not before we make arrangements to meet three weeks hence, when Buddy and I are due back in Moscow from Latvia, where I hope to get permission to visit Dvinsk, the city my father was born in which is also closed to foreigners. As it happened, we were granted a one-day pass.

The next time, Rita brings Anna and young Mark, aged fourteen — small for his age with tousled curly red hair and an irresistible smile, as well as their own interpreter. Able at last to talk freely, Rita starts to fill in some bits and pieces of our family history.

After they were married in 1920, Faina moved to Viatka with Uncle Mark, where she "enjoyed" the displeasure of the Steiman family until they left for Canada in 1924. Try as they would to convince Mark to emigrate with them, Solomon and Etza were no match for Faina, who was not about to pack up and leave Russia and her family to move to an unknown country to live with in-laws who hadn't a kind word for her. I can hear her saying, "No, let them go. We're staying right here in Viatka," planning all the while to get Mark to move to Nizhny-Novgorod, which she soon succeeded in doing.

Nizhny-Novgorod, situated at the point where the Volga River meets the Oka, is an ancient city, founded in the thirteenth century. Because of its advantageous geographic position, it had become a major commercial and cultural centre. Its annual trade fair was legendary, attracting merchants from all over Russia and Central Asia. It is likely that Grandfather Solomon had attended these fairs as a representative of the H.W. Böker Company. With the forced evacuation of the Jews from within the Pale of Settlement in 1915 and the abandonment of the Pale laws entirely during the post-war revolutionary period, the Jewish population of this historic city increased from 2,327 in 1897 to 9,328 thirty years later, and among the recent arrivals were the Frierman family from Mogilev. Nizhny-Novgorod was a culturally vibrant city, being the birthplace of the mathematician Nikolai Lobachevsky, the composer Mili Balakirev and the writer Maxim Gorky, and had much more to offer in the way of theatre, opera, art and education than Viatka ever would. So it is understandable that Faina, whose brother Ruveim was a member of

Mara and Mark Steiman,
Viatka, USSR, 1925

the new revolutionary "intelligentsia," would choose to return there rather than live "in exile" elsewhere.

By the time Nizhny-Novgorod was renamed Gorky in 1936, Faina, always strong-willed, domineering and impossible to please, had become increasingly difficult to live with. She basked in her brother Ruveim's growing fame as a writer. His first novel had appeared in 1924 and was followed by many stories addressed mainly to teenage readers. Later, his fifth novel, published in 1939, *Dingo — The Wild Dog* — or *First Love*, would become a best-seller, read widely in high schools throughout the Soviet Union and later made into a popular film. Indeed, Faina now felt that she had married beneath her, that she deserved more than an easy-going, good-natured bookkeeper for a husband. In consequence, she and Mark began to drift apart, until one day he was swept away entirely by a fair-haired, *zaftig* (full-bodied, "juicy") Russian woman with a nature as sweet as the candy she dispensed over the counter of the state-owned confectionery shop where they both worked. There is no doubt that Mark hated leaving Mara, whom he dearly loved, but she was now sixteen and would soon embark upon a life of her own.

One can only hope that he found some comfort in his new relationship, because when the Germans invaded Russia in 1941, Mark was called up once more and at age forty-one, with weak lungs, was passed as fit and sent to the front as cannon fodder. Faina, now almost fifty, found herself again working in a military hospital. In 1942, Faina received word that Mark had been killed in action — no further details were given. His body was never found. And so she joined the ranks of millions of Russian war widows. No one ever spoke of the fate of Uncle Mark's Russian sweetheart.

As a young girl, Mara joined the Pioneers (Communist party organization for children ten to sixteen years of age) and later became a leader in the Komsomol (for Young Communist party members sixteen years of age and older), which was the key to getting ahead in the Soviet system. (Whether Uncle Mark and Aunt Faina were also ardent Communists, I don't know, but I suspect that at least Faina was.) After graduating with a degree in economics from the technological college in Gorky, Mara got a job in the oldest and largest automobile factory, Gorky being the Detroit of the Soviet Union. She was twenty in 1941 when the war broke out and took an active part in the prodigious Komsomol war effort. She helped organize and co-ordinate the Komsomol brigades. Thousands of young people, mainly girls, since all able-bodied men were at the front, were organized in each district to help people in distress, to dig trenches, chop wood, pile sandbags, look after orphaned children, and when the Germans started to bomb the city to destroy the tank factory and other essential industries, they helped with evacuation arrangements.

But even during these terrible days, life went on. People fell in love and got married. Mara met Leonid Skorupsky, a young Jewish radiologist at the military hospital, whom she married in 1944. Shortly thereafter, together with Faina, they followed the relocation of their military hospital to Ivano-

Frankovsk in the Ukraine, where the three of them shared a twenty-three-square-meter flat in an old, one-storey barracks-like building. It had no running water or indoor toilet facilities and they shared a kitchen with two other families. It was there, in July 1945, that their daughter Margarita was born.

Almost coincidental with the birth of her baby, it became apparent that Mara had developed a severe and crippling disease. Leonid attempted to get the best treatment for her, even though medical facilities were overcrowded and medicines in short supply. He took her to many sanatoria and to Black Sea spas in an effort to restore her health, but without success.

In the meantime, living in a small apartment with Faina's temper tantrums and mood-swings was beginning to have its effect. Leonid could not please his mother-in-law Faina, no matter how hard he tried. So one day in 1950, while he was at work, Faina packed up her daughter Mara and her granddaughter Rita, now five, and returned to Gorky, where they moved into equally cramped quarters. Eventually, after six or seven years, they got a one-bedroom apartment with a kitchen all their own.

Faina, now nearly sixty, became even more difficult, embittered and nervous. She was scraping by on her war widow's small pension of fifty rubles a month, which she augmented by working as guard in a school. She had become one of the ubiquitous *babushkas*, the tough breed of older women in the Soviet Union who had survived two world wars, a revolution and a counter-revolutionary war, and who now ruled fiercely over a world of cloakrooms, broom closets and ticket offices and who swept the streets and cleaned the halls of vast public buildings and hospitals.

Life was not easy for Mara either. Designated an "invalid of the second class," she had difficulty finding work. At last she got a job as a record-keeper in a sewing factory at a salary of thirty rubles a month. As opposed to her mother, however, Mara was grateful for any opportunity, because invalids of the second class are usually considered unemployable.

The child Rita, a pretty blond with blue-grey eyes and curly hair, was brought up in this sordid, almost Dickensian household, by her termagant grandma and crippled mother. As the years passed, both Faina's and Mara's health continued to degenerate. There were days Mara could barely drag herself down to her job. Gorky was closed to foreigners at the time Laura and Iser came to Russia in 1962 and Mara was too sick to go to Moscow, even had she been able to get the necessary travel permit. Young Rita was writing examinations and running back and forth to the hospital where Faina was dying.

In due course, Rita graduated from high school, studied at the Gorky Auto School for three years and was given work as a dispatcher at the Gorky Auto Parts Depot. All the while, Mara's health continued to deteriorate. At fifty-three, she looked like an old woman of seventy. In 1972 she was so crippled and ill she could not attend Rita's wedding to Shmuel Konkolsky, a Jewish electrician. Rita gave birth to Anna in 1973 and the next year, Mara died. Her last request was that Rita name her son, if she had one, Mark. In 1975, Rita did. But four years later her marriage ended in divorce.

Margarita Konkolsky, Gorky, USSR, 1968

My curiosity satisfied at last, Rita, Anna and I (Mark just listens) go on to discuss the possibility of their immigrating to Canada. Had Great-uncle Robert Steiman been alive (he died in 1954 at the age of eighty-one), he would have taken the initiative to get the last of our family out of Russia. But he is not. Somehow, I have inherited his legacy in this regard. Obviously, it's in the blood. She is not eligible to immigrate under the family reunification category. She is too distant a relation. The likelihood of her finding work in her field at her age is slim. But there may be a way. Nothing, however, is decided. The Konkolskys return to Gorky, Buddy and I to Vancouver.

Back home in Gorky, Rita wonders and waits. Wonders if she should take the chance of emigrating to Canada, based on the assurances of . . . relatives, yes, but otherwise complete strangers met once. Waiting to see if there is actually anything concrete worth wondering about. She is sorely tempted. Almost every Jew in the Soviet Union is affected by exodus fever. Anyone who has the remotest relative or friend in the West is trying to get out or, at the very least, visit the West. And there is the lesson of her grandfather and grandmother, Mark and Faina, who missed their chance back in 1924.

THE LAST OF OUR MOHICANS

On the other hand, several of Rita's friends and a couple of distant relatives had emigrated to Israel in the EXODUS program and written back that the situation there was not all roses. Besides, life in Gorky, she feels, isn't all that bad. She has received a promotion and raise at the Gorky Auto Parts Depot where she works and every year enjoys a month's holiday at her factory's workers' resort in Sochi on the Crimean Riviera. True, food is scarce and rationed and pollution has reached monumental proportions with Gorky's factories spewing so much waste into the Oka River that the fish pulled out and sold at the market are grotesquely deformed. Meat, green vegetables, tomatoes, they see only in their dreams. They are not starving on their diet of bread, potatoes and macaroni, but Mark suffers from a stomach disorder never clearly diagnosed.

Her children are relatively happy at school. Anna will graduate from high school next year. Mark, blessed with perfect pitch, plays the trumpet and sings in an *a capella* choir. What if all this immigration business is a pipe dream? What if all that happens is that she and her children are brought to the attention of the KGB? What then?

Once again, Russian Jews are caught in a classic Catch-22. As long as the USSR will not let Jews out, they are welcome in the West. As soon as the Gorbachev regime agrees to their emigration, however, they cannot get into any country — except Israel. And the consequences of applying to emigrate, if unsuccessful, could be dire.

Finally, the moment of decision: Vulf Sternin, my designated interpreter-interlocutor in Vancouver, phones Rita in January 1990 to tell her (in perfect Russian) that she and her two children can come to Canada as visitors and apply for landed immigrant status once here. As this policy is under revision and likely soon to be rescinded, this is their only chance. He assures her that Buddy and I are willing to sign a legal and binding "invitation" agreeing to support them in every way for the duration (of their visit and until they become landed immigrants), so that they will not become a charge on the Canadian government. Even so she has doubts. She's old. At forty-three she fears she'll never learn English. Vulf also tells her that he had made the same decision ten years earlier for his son's sake and had not regretted it, and that she should think about the futures of Anna and Mark. On the basis of his advice and the fact that time is running out, she finally decides to take the plunge.

Under Vulf Sternin's guidance from afar, Rita begins "the fiction" of her three-month visit to Canada. First, she has to obtain a leave of absence from her work. Second, she has to obtain clearance from the Gorky Metropolitan Police. Third, KGB clearance. Fourth, she has to apply for passports and visas. Fifth, she, Anna and Mark have to pass medicals. All of which is difficult enough in any country, but in the USSR, is also fraught with endless bureaucratic frustration and delay. Sixth, she has to sell everything, including "squatter's rights" to her cramped, twenty-seven-square-meter apartment.

The scarcity of apartments in Gorky meant that all kinds of subterfuges had been developed to circumvent bureaucratic procedures. If Rita simply left the country, abandoning her apartment, the state would take it over without compensation and allot it to whoever was next on the waiting list, or to whoever had bribed the housing official the most. In consequence, Rita arranges for a friend to move in a week before she is to leave. He will "squat" there, pay the minimal rent to the authorities and lay claim to it when the state discovers Rita has left the country for good. For this he pays her four thousand rubles, the equivalent of four hundred dollars, and she is allowed to take out three hundred dollars.

Between the rubles we are sending her via a friend in Riga (who has a seemingly endless, inexpensive supply), the sale of all her household and personal possessions and the "sale" of her apartment, Rita suddenly finds herself rich. Really rich — Russian style.

Now, however, she fears the jealousy and wrath of her neighbours. She fears robbery. She fears for her life and the lives of her children. Relative poverty is all she has ever known — living with Mara and Faina on their small pensions, then later living on wages of one hundred and fifty rubles a month. Suddenly, and ironically, when she is about to leave Russia, she is ruble rich. Fortunately perhaps, "ruble rich" means one has a lot of money, but there is nothing to buy. Consequently, she has little choice other than to live as usual and this keeps her safe.

What really causes her heartache, and toothache as it turns out, is a small gold dish — her inheritance from her ardent Communist grandmother, Faina! Gold cannot be taken out of the USSR. The authorities are likely to become quite nasty if one is caught trying to do so. Rita, however, is unwilling either to sell it or leave it behind. She decides to smuggle it out on her teeth, gold crowns and caps being all the rage in Gorky. The telephone lines over the thousands of miles that separate us burn red hot when she tells Vulf of her plans, which he in turn relays to me. Russian dentistry is notoriously poor and performed without anaesthetic. Don't do it. Gold teeth are not fashionable in the West. Don't do it on any account. Make buttons, bracelets, anything but teeth.

Six months, countless phone calls and letters later, Rita and the children are ready, all their papers in order. Rita travels to Chernigov in the Ukraine to see her father, perhaps for the last time. A distinguished-looking man, a retired radiologist now in his eighties, he is happy that she has the opportunity to leave, regrets that he is too old to start a new life. They pose for a last photo and Rita returns to Gorky to discover one more hitch: a two-year waiting list for tickets on the Soviet airline, Aeroflot. Again the classic Catch-22: a Soviet citizen can't get a ticket without a visitor's visa from the appropriate foreign government, but the visa will expire before the ticket is valid! Meanwhile, Canada is in the process of closing her doors to the sort of immigration procedure we are counting on to bring the last of the Steiman Mohicans into the bosom of their extended family. What to do?

For hard currency, we discover everything is possible in the USSR. With the help of a friendly travel agent in Vancouver, we purchase three return tickets on an Aeroflot flight from Moscow to Amsterdam; and three more from KLM to ferry them the rest of the way. Return tickets were part of the fiction required by both the Soviet and Canadian governments, as well as a fallback for us, just in case they were crazy enough to want to go back. As they sit in plush upholstered seats, listening to canned music, watching movies, being served butter with their bread, enjoying fresh baked salmon, endless coffee, tea, milk and Coca-Cola by smiling stewardesses, their trip across the Atlantic is a far cry from Robert Steiman's long voyage, steerage-class, in 1899. In fact, for Rita, Anna and Mark, KLM's Flying Dutchman was more like a magic carpet whirling them away from the land of an evil giant that had kept her and her children captive for years — to the safe haven that Canada has been for so many of our family.

They land in Vancouver on a perfect blue-green afternoon in July — only ten days short of Rita's 45th birthday, re-birthday actually. The Vancouver International Airport was a madhouse, as usual. We are all there. My husband Buddy, son Gary, daughter Connie and her husband John and our grandson, Graeme. Friends Vulf and Maya Sternin are on hand to interpret and most significantly, Doris Gould, daughter of the first Steiman to arrive in Canada in

1899. Anna and Mark come through the swinging glass doors looking tense and tired. Rita follows, searching the crowd through thick-lensed glasses. I run up, arms outstretched. She steps forward to greet me, her smile glittering and golden.

As soon as they recovered from jet lag, culture shock set in. Where else should this happen but in the vast Superstore only a short distance from their apartment, where we had gone, interpreter in tow, to purchase the basic necessities of life in the New World. Once inside, they were astounded by the sights, the sounds, the smells and the size; it was so big the stock boys were roller-skating up and down the aisles. The family needed milk. We showed them 1%,

Marion Katz and Doris Gould, daughters of Robert (the first Steiman to come to Canada), with Margarita, centre, Anna and Mark Konkolsky, Vancouver, July 1991

2%, homogenized and skim, buttermilk and chocolate milk in 1/2, 1 and 2-litre cartons and in 4-litre plastic jugs. Eggs, the interpreter pointed out, came in extra-large, large, medium and small, brown or white, in packages of 6, 12 or 24. There were 27 kinds of bread, but no familiar black bread. As we sauntered up and down the aisles, we were all suddenly overcome by the towering abundance of absolutely everything. Toilet paper, which I remember was non-existent in public facilities in Russia, was displayed here in a variety of qualities: 1-ply, 2-ply, 3-ply, utility, soft and super-soft, recycled and non-recycled, in colours and prints. Totally bewildered, Rita asked, "How can I decide?"

I paused to consider. "These decisions are easy," I finally told her. "Soon you'll be choosing a prime minister!"

The next morning Rita and her children walked to the Superstore on their own, and every morning thereafter this excursion became part of their daily routine. Like anthropologists studying a strange new culture, they examined minutely everything on the shelves, every day reassuring themselves that it was not a dream. In the spring of 1991, another dream came true. Rita,

Mark and Anna sat at our dining-room table and, with Mark asking the four questions in Russian, they celebrated Passover for the first time in their lives.

And finally, in 1995, a third dream was realized. With all the pomp and ceremony befitting the occasion, amidst smiles and tears and handshakes of congratulations, the last of our Mohicans became proud Canadian citizens.

Margarita Konkolsky, proud Canadian citizen, Vancouver, 1995

Bibliography

The following books were invaluable guides in my journey of discovery:

Abella, Irving. *A Coat of Many Colours: Two Centuries of Jewish Life in Canada.* Toronto, Lester and Orpen Dennys Ltd., 1990.

Belkin, Simon. *Through Narrow Gates.* Montreal: Canadian Jewish Congress, 1966.

Dimont, M.I. *Jews, God and History.* New York: Simon and Schuster Inc., 1964.

Dubnow, S.M. *History of the Jews in Russia and Poland.* 3 vols. Philadelphia: The Jewish Publication Society, 1920.

Flior, Yudel. *Dvinsk: The Rise and Decline of a Town.* Johannesburg: Dial Press.

Gitelman, Zvi. *A Century of Ambivalence: The Jews of Russian and the Soviet Union.* New York: Schocken Books, 1986.

Greenberg, Louis. *The Jews in Russia.* Yale University Press, 1965.

Gutkiön, H. *Journey Into Our Heritage: The Story of the Jewish People in the Canadian West.* Toronto: Lester and Orpen Dennys Ltd., 1980.

Howe, Irving. *The World of Our Fathers.* New York: Harcourt Brace Jovanovich Inc., 1976.

Kamsack History Book Society. *Spinning Stories: A Woven History.* Regina, Saskatchewan: Focus, 1988.

Malkin, Carole. *The Journeys of David Toback.* New York: Schocken Books, 1981.

Philipson, D. *Old European Jewries.* Philadelphia: The Jewish Publications Society, 1894.

Rybakov, Anatoli. *Children of the Arbat.* New York: Little, Brown, 1988.

Werth, A. *Russia at War, 1941-45.* London: Barrie & Radcliffe, 1964.

UNIVERSITY OF CALGARY PRESS

A FAMILY CHRONICLE

MENDEL'S CHILDREN

by

CHERIE SMITH

ISBN 1-895176-85-9 $19.95

Shipping: Canada $5.00; International $9.00

Canadian orders add 7% GST.
Outside Canada, prices are in U.S. dollars.

METHOD OF PAYMENT

Payment or purchase order must accompany order.
Please make cheque payable to **UBC Press**.

❑ Cheque ❑ Money Order ❑ Mastercard ❑ Visa

Credit Card Number _____

Expiry Date _____
(Credit card not valid without expiry date.)

SHIPPING INSTRUCTIONS

Name _____
Address _____
_____
City _____
Province/State _____
Postal/Zip Code _____
Country _____

University of Calgary Press Web: www.ucalgary.ca/ucpress

Please send orders to:

UBC Press, University of British Columbia
6344 Memorial Road
Vancouver, B.C., Canada V6T 1Z2
Telephone: (604) 822-5959
From Canada or U.S.A., fax orders to: 1-800-668-0821
Outside Canada and U.S.A., fax orders to: (604) 822-6083

UC
PRESS